THE SILICON SOCIETY

Is high technology growing out of control, or can we shape it before it shapes us?

We are living through the decade of the information revolution. Robots at work, home computers and micro-processor-controlled devices at home, computer-controlled missiles and defence systems — the silicon chip has brought all these from the dream of the early 1970s to the reality of today. And we are soon to encounter the 'artificial intelligence' of fifth-generation computers.

Dr David Lyon is studying the social aspects of information technology as a research fellow at Leeds University, England. This is also a theme of his lecturing in social analysis at Bradford and Ilkley College. This book continues the quest of his previous books, for a genuinely human way ahead for technological society. He has written *Karl Marx: an assessment of his life and thought*; *Sociology and the Human Image*; *Future Society*; and *The Steeple's Shadow: the myths and realities of secularization*. Dr Lyon has held a visiting professorship in Canada and a research fellowship in the United States. He is married with four children.

For
André et Laurence
David and Pam
Geraint and Mary
John and Sarah
Nick and Judy
Sander en Dorine
all faithful friends

THE SILICON SOCIETY

DAVID LYON

WM. B. EERDMANS
PUBLISHING CO.
Grand Rapids, Michigan

This American edition published 1986 by
William B. Eerdmans Publishing Company,
255 Jefferson S.E., Grand Rapids,
Michigan 49503, USA

First edition published in the UK 1986
by Lion Publishing plc

ISBN 0 8028 0238 9

This book contains the substance of the London
Lectures in Contemporary Christianity 1985. The
London Lectures were founded in 1974. Their
purpose is to develop biblical Christian thinking on
the issues of the day. They are delivered annually,
in association with the London Institute for
Contemporary Christianity, which is located in
St Peter's Church, Vere Street, London W1.
Neither the Council of the London Institute nor
the London Lectures Committee necessarily
endorses all the views that the lecturers express.

Printed and bound in Great Britain by
Cox and Wyman, Reading

CONTENTS

Introduction

What's in a question mark? The lectures on which this book is based were entitled 'Silicon Society?'. I wanted to indicate two things. First, that the social changes associated with the 'silicon chip' are huge, and far-reaching. Second, that they raise questions and prompt critique.

So the issue of how the chip will change our lives is only half the story. Although I am convinced that much of the chip's impact is beneficial, we must not be blinkered and ignore its other effects. This book is largely about the other effects. Allowing new technology to shape society is one thing. How we should shape new technology is another. The two sides of the story must be kept together.

Do not be misled by dire predictions about doom in the computer industry, or crises in new communications. These are but the ups and downs of brand new technologies. Some companies do collapse, some innovations do fall by the wayside. But the overall trends are unmistakable. Information technology is rapidly becoming a key to the future development of the world economy.

This book touches on many areas affected by new technology. First, we set the scene, by looking at what is meant by the 'second industrial revolution'. Second, we examine what computer automation means for the world of work, skill, and (un)employment. Farms, factories and offices are all affected. In some cases, we find people working from home, in the 'electronic cottage'. The new telecommunications make such 'homeworking' possible. But this aspect of new technology also has many other implications — cable TV, satellite broadcasting, new data networks — which are the subject of the third chapter.

The arrival in the real world of robots linked with 'artificial intelligence' raises another range of questions. As machines become more like humans, will they take over our decisions? Are we creating a 'computer culture'? Chapter Four explores these questions, leaving the final chapter to comment on new technology and 'Big Brother'. Will democracy be helped or hindered? If digital data can be so easily 'zapped', what will happen to 'truth' in political and social life?

Apart from the last issue mentioned, none is 'new' to information technology. They are questions we have had to face before. But they hit us hard today for four important reasons. The pace of change is quickening. All aspects of life are affected at once. The consequences are long-term, and they are global. This is why their consideration is so urgent.

Part of my task, then, is *analysis*. What exactly is going on, and why? Although I am an enthusiastic user of new technology (word processing, databases, and so on), social analysis, not new technology, is my particular calling. Patient friends, mentioned below, have helped me understand the operation and significance of new technology. Patient readers will, I hope, forgive mistakes I have still made.

The other part of my task is *evaluation*. This is an *ethical* task, in which we ask further questions of new technology: what is it for? who will benefit? who decides? Sadly, new technology is often presented to us as the only way forward, as if there were no choices. I challenge this, and ask that we all be involved in making these crucial choices. For new technology affects all our lives.

You may well ask, 'how *do* we develop new technology for a humane world?' How do we know what is for the best? I lay my cards on the table at this point. My evaluation is rooted in the tradition of Jewish-Christian thought. I say *'Jewish-*Christian' to emphasize that the Old Testament still has much to say to us. Jesus frequently invoked its wisdom as the way forward for his own followers. You must read on to discover what I mean.

In giving the original lectures (in November 1985) I felt the force of criticism from two directions. Some thought I was too optimistic about new technology. I was warned that the world would simply become less and less hospitable to humans. Others disagreed. New technology would liberate us for leisure and for worthwhile pursuits in a more caring society. I am glad that each thought me mistaken. Readers must judge for themselves!

I have never struggled to hold down an over-eager hot-air balloon. But trying to draw together in one place all the strands of 'new technology and human life' feels just like that must do. It may appear an ambitious task. But because the issues are so important, and because properly ethical practice is at such a low premium, I offer my contribution.

I am extremely grateful to members of the Shaftesbury Project Information Technology Study Group, plus some other friends, all named below. Through critical discussion and encouragement, they shared with me the burden of preparation, and contributed in numerous ways to the shape of the lectures. They are: Howard Davis, Jen Dening, Dirk de Vos, David Field, Arthur Francis, Mark Gregory, Mike LeRoy, Paul MacDonald, Roy McCloughry, David Martin, John Mullaley, Michael Parsons, Miriam Sampson, Quin Schultze, Egbert Schuurman and John Stott.

Thanks are due to the Committee of the London Lectures in Contemporary Christianity for inviting me to give the lectures, and also to the keenly responsive audience who on successive Monday nights pushed me to clarify and qualify what I had said. I have tried to take account of some of those debates in the final text.

During the lectures our children patiently and encouragingly put up with an especially busy and preoccupied Dad. My precious partner and keen critic, Sue, has supported me as only she knows how. When the snow comes, we'll all go sledging. When the spring comes, we'll all go cycling, I promise.

1
The silicon scenario

Just a few years ago, Santa Clara County in California was mainly famous for its fruit. Then the breakthrough into micro-electronics established a new reputation for this orchard country — as 'Silicon Valley'. By the early 1980s, not only had everyone heard about the amazing miniaturization of electronic circuits, but because of their plummeting costs, millions of people were already being affected by them in their everyday lives.

The 'silicon chip' has made possible the huge 'information technology' boom which began in the late 1970s. What had been the technology of the elite has become, in principle, a technology for the mass. Computers of rapidly shrinking size seem to appear everywhere: railway marshalling yards, car dashboards, kitchens, schools, office desks and government departments. But computers are only half the information technology (IT) story. The other half is that they are now linked together by telephone lines and television cables, within offices, across continents, and indeed span the globe.

Since the start of Silicon Valley, similar centres of university plus high technology enterprise have sprung up around places such as Route 128 outside Boston, along the M4 motorway in Britain, on the German autobahn between Nuremberg and Munich, and round Toulouse in France. The British boast a 'Silicon Fen' round Cambridge, and a 'Silicon Glen' in central Scotland. Many believe that a new day has dawned for the human race, and that first light is appearing from these 'sunrise' industries. Robert Noyce, co-inventor of the integrated circuit (chip) said: 'A true revolution: a qualitative change in technology . . . has given rise to a qualitative change in human capabilities.' Not only that, but Silicon Valley 'holds the keys to the kingdom'.[1]

This book is about the 'silicon revolution', not so much in the technical sense of what machines can now do, important though that is, but more in the sense of how the chip changes our lives. Will the chip reduce jobs and take the skill out of work even as it multiplies brain power? Will IT isolate us at our computer terminals even as it connects us together by new telecommunications?

But even these questions are not the most significant ones. If we only think of new technology as 'arriving', so that we now have to cope with it, and make the best of it, we have allowed ourselves to be blinded by it. To understand it, we must see where it came from, how its origins shaped it. Take the 'Silicon Valley' phenomenon. It was conceived when Americans, worried by the Cold War threat seen in the launch of the Russian 'sputnik', realized that defence of the future would depend on miniaturization of components. Government support was given to micro-electronics in order to supply the California aerospace industry. As we shall see, we cannot afford to ignore the chip's parentage.

Once we perceive that new technology does not just arrive, perhaps from a boffin's brainwave, but that it results from human choices, economic pressures, and political ideologies, we can begin to get it in perspective. By thus taking a little of the magic out of the 'mighty micro' we are in a better position to evaluate it. Rather than simply assuming that new technology is with us for better or worse, we can begin to see how different kinds of choices could affect the eventual direction of technological development.

This brings us to the other distinctive feature of this book. IT will not itself usher in a leisured society where robots take the toil out of work and new telecommunications provide endless opportunities for entertainment. The benefits will not come automatically. Do we want to grapple with the real meaning and actual developments in IT? To resist the rise of 'Big Brother'? To ensure that all who could benefit from IT do so? If we are to shape the new technology before it shapes us, then we need a clear idea of where we want to go.

The conviction expressed here is that Christian faith may be applied sensitively to the contemporary world of new technology. It promises no slick solutions but does offer a badly-needed sense of direction. Christianity's high view of human potential to invent and to create (our affinity with the Creator) leads us to support the drive towards new technologies as a means of opening the earth's resources to all. This means that however critical we might have to be about the way technology is developed, our attitude towards 'doing technology' is fundamentally positive. But with this comes a realism which cautions us to expect that some technological developments will be misguided and mistaken, just because the humans involved in their creation are far from perfect. This does not mean that we are simply cynical pessimists. The Christian message is one of hope, that through an acceptance of God's initiative in Jesus we may discover what it really means to be human, and work it out in everyday life. It is a short step from here to seeing how technology itself may be humanized, to serve the purposes of justice, peace, and ecology.

Another industrial revolution?

Since the start of televising at the House of Lords, the British public have become aware that their lordships often refer to a 'second industrial revolution'. Unlike the original process, which was not a 'revolution' until so dubbed by historians, this is a revolution for which we are urged to prepare and plan. Witness also the writing on new technology and society by politicians such as British Social Democratic Party President Shirley Williams (*A Job to Live*[2]), Australian Labour Minister Barry Jones (*Sleepers Awake!*[3]), or the Canadian government publication: *Planning Now for an Information Society: Tomorrow Is Too Late*.[4]

The idea is that the changes through which we are now going are every bit as tremendous as those which transformed the world of local communities based on subsistence agriculture into the world of sprawling cities, machines, mills, and factories. Now it is said that the world is dying. A new one, structured round services and the handling, sending, and exploiting for power of information by electronic means, is being born.

If the symbolic figure of industrial society was the urban factory worker, then his or her future equivalent is the more leisured, casually-dressed, computer-literate manipulator of digital information. This could be the business consultant, airline clerk, or fashion editor, each of whom may as easily work from home as in a central office. (Indeed, one may now observe peripatetic information workers hunched over their portable computers in the seats of the high speed trains.)

Needless to say, no one planned for industrial society, which has now been reproduced around the world, because no one predicted its arrival in the way that the information society is expected today. Things have changed. The emphasis, at least the *technical* emphasis, has shifted to the future, and is forecast and discussed long before it arrives. So we are deluged with fanciful futuristic figments such as the electronic cottage, computer democracy, and the paperless office. But how realistic are such dreams?

For Mrs Sharon Jones, who sits at her computer terminal in Maryland nine hours a day, feeding the machine with un-inspiring data (Blue Shield medical insurance claims), the electronic cottage seems more like a prison. According to *The New York Times*, who reported her case, she works uncom-plainingly. Excluded from the company of colleagues, yet often obliged to earn to support children, women such as Mrs Jones wait in vain for technological liberation.[5] For the flexitime professional, on the other hand, who chooses her workplace, and uses the computer to enhance her creativity, the outlook may be a lot more rosy.

Whatever the pundits say, new technology will not itself bring about a new society. We must explore the connection between the *potential* of the new technology and the existing social, political and economic arrangements in which it is developing.

Recently, one of the strongest spurs to feverish activity in micro-electronics has been the Japanese promise of 'fifth generation' computers by the 1990s. Such is the faith in the future with IT that all the advanced nations have been falling over themselves to ward off what they see as a Japanese threat. We shall comment later on the meaning of the 'fifth generation'. It is the underlying impetus I wish to highlight here: the future is seen in terms of competing to build a supercomputer. The stress is on *how?*, not *why?*.

Nations are planning for the second industrial revolution, and its putative partner, the information society. The Japanese have a clear notion of where they are going, plus the drive, co-ordination and political consensus to get there. Their high-tech civilization is already moving from drawing board to concrete reality. France also realized, early on, the desirability of a plan of action which co-ordinated computing and telecommunications. And although the 'silicon scenario' has in the USA largely been orchestrated by industry, the defence department and the media, government plans and attitudes play a part. In Britain innovation in fields such as videotex, fibre optics, and software, plus the 'free play of market forces' and wide-ranging initiatives — for example, information technology centres, 'ITeCs' — are appealed to as ways of guaranteeing future growth or, more pessimistically, of avoiding demotion to 'Third World' status.

But how appropriate is all this? Our modern culture, with its belief in a line of progress which stretches to the horizon, obliges us to construct goals, or have them made for us, like 'information society'. Then all attention is concentrated on reaching the goal. But the mammoth social changes which IT seems to hold in store provide an incentive for us to stop and ask ourselves where we really want to go.

The very idea of planning for a new society expresses the over-confident spirit of our age. Although it is important not to lose sight of the wider dimensions and 'knock-on effects' of new technology in other areas of society, we would do well to focus on specific issues. IT is likely to affect the future shape and direction of institutions such as families, factories, churches, libraries, and governments. Once we have examined IT in today's society, we shall be in a better position to ask what sort of changes would be desirable, and what we want to avoid.

Information technology in today's society

Perhaps you wonder why so much fuss is made about IT. Is not technology always altering and advancing? What is different about IT, and why will it make such dramatic changes to our way of life?

● **IT is a 'heartland' technology.** That is, the introduction of the chip affects numerous other areas of production, organization, and communication. The combination of miniaturization and vastly reduced costs makes possible hitherto undreamed-of applications.

The efficiency of our local foodstores is increased by putting bar codes (those little black and white stripes) on cornflakes packets. The computerized information — that they are down to the last carton — can be fed directly into stock control and trigger the reordering process. The same technology gets rid of all the grubby index cards in the library, and also summons us back to the library immediately a book is overdue. And if these machines can 'read' the little plastic strips, then others can 'read' even more complex forms of data, such as documents. This in turn contributes to the computerization of another workplace, the office.

As the list grows, it becomes clear that few areas of life are likely to be immune from the impacts of IT. I am a grateful user of the word processor, which radically affects my toil as a writer. I used to scrawl out a rough copy on old paper, commit a subsequent draft to the typewriter, scribble marginalia, score out and insert new matter, then start again with the typewriter. After a while those freshly-typed sheets would be cut up and pasted together in different combinations until I was happy with the result (or despaired of making things any better).

Now I can sketch the original ideas, make draft after draft, cut, paste and edit electronically without using any paper, before making a printed copy, or numerous copies, from the machine. And the process of finding something to write about is similarly eased using the same machine as a straight computer. It will store notes and references once kept in an index file, and sort them into alphabetical order, to be retrieved when I want them. For some purposes researchers no longer have to visit the British Museum or Bibliotheque Nationale to pore over dusty journals. Via the computer terminal in the library (and at a price!) I can call up a distant 'database' (a sort of computerized library of information). To help me write this I called up *Dialog* in California to discover, for example, what has been written about the social effects of turning fruit orchards into Silicon Valley.

Doctors use computers for speed and accuracy of diagnosis. Machine tools for cutting metal are controlled by computer. Computers also aid their design. Link computers up by telephone, datalines, or TV cables and people are enabled to shop, to bank, to work or be educated at home. Blight on crops, the presence of fish shoals, or the buildup of weather systems is sensed, remotely, using computers — the results of the latter being what we see on the TV screen each night.

Thus as the power of computing is yoked together with new telecommunications the potential reach of IT is apparently limitless.

● **IT raises questions of power.** Before writing had been developed, people stored information in their heads, and shared it by talking. Folk-tales, songs, and ancient wisdom were repeated in the field and by the hearth. They were tremendously important for keeping the community together, for ensuring that hunting skills were passed on, or for knowing why the chief was to be obeyed. Whether by marks on cave walls or by complex Egyptian hieroglyphs, the coming of writing meant that information could be stored and disseminated far more easily. Etching the Ten Commandments in stone gave them a permanence that oral rules could never possess. Writing also put non-readers and non-writers at a comparative disadvantage. Now they were at the mercy of those with the powerful pen.

The invention of printing boosted the production and dissemination of information. Printed matter became part of the stuff of political life, and could have either a repressive or a liberating quality. Expressed in the rule-book of a bureaucratic organization, the written word can tie you down. But expressed in the pamphlet, the novel, even the Bible itself, the word may show a path different to that recommended by the powers-that-be.

In the later twentieth century we are witnessing a massive shift towards *electronic* means of storing, retrieving, and disseminating information. If mechanized printing conditioned what forms of information were available and who could use them, how much more will new technology open or close our choices? Some believe, following Marshall McLuhan, that a decentralized, participatory paradise will be created by the electronic media. Others, who share George Orwell's fears, see in the police national computer (at Hendon, England) or in the computerized mass-mailing methods of the American New Right, the death knell of liberty.

Later, we shall look at computers and control in the workplace, and at new telecommunications (such as cable TV) and political power. Right now, let us simply note that information handling is crucial to power in society. New media deeply affect the world they help organize.

● **The pace of technological change has accelerated**. Driven by commercial motivations and political pressures, a new pattern of development is now apparent. Previous changes have depended largely on inventions — Jethro Tull's seed drill or James Watts' steam engine, for example. The tides of today's technology incorporate a new dimension: research laboratories. No 'invisible hand' guides new technology as economists once thought. Rather, industry's systematic research programmes, supported via universities by governments (especially in defence-related spheres) are the seed-beds of new technology. New products are launched as soon as they are thought to be economically feasible.

This means that the gap between discovery and production

has dramatically narrowed. World War II heralded a sudden upturn in science and technology in the advanced societies, not least because the war's outcome depended in part on new technology: radar, radio, and computers. This accelerated pace of change is clearly visible in the Japanese 'fifth generation' project which in the early 1980s promised that by the 1990s 'artificial intelligence' would be firmly and competitively established.

This is the main reason why anticipating and planning for future society has risen so high on the agenda (though some argue that we have already allowed technological change to become uncontrollable). In Britain this means that the government is constantly under attack for cutting back on its pioneering micro-electronics education programme, for failing to support basic research and development in IT, and for allowing a shortfall of highly-qualified graduates with high-tech expertise. The pace of change has quickened.

The result is that technology is fast outstripping the pace of political and social adjustment. Having accepted that IT is the only way forward we are now in danger of letting it slip beyond our control. In our generation we have seen the Swiss watch industry decimated by digital watches from Japan and the USA. People fear for their jobs and their work quality as robots and word processors are installed. We are watching global rifts widen daily as the North's research and development romps forward, leaving the South technologically further and further behind. The armaments race — especially the 'Star Wars' programme — is fuelled by blind faith in technological 'superiority' and technological fixes for political problems, thus perpetuating the belief that IT offers solutions.

Given these three factors — that IT is a heartland technology, with huge implications for power, and a speeding rate of change, we come to realize we have opened a Pandora's box. In fact, it has been open for a long time. Things *seem* out of control. But if we think that means we can do nothing, then we ignore another crucial dimension: technology is a *human construction*.

Technology is a human construction

As we have seen, the arrival of IT at this point in history is no accident. A significant French government report by Nora and Minc says, *'L'informatisation'* (which means 'computerization *plus* telecommunications') is 'a key issue in the French crisis'. IT is eagerly sought as an antidote for world recession, lack of competitiveness, and a falling rate of profit.

No accident; a 'human construction'. This is illustrated by the fact that technology develops in different ways in different contexts. Why does the Soviet Union refuse to allow the spread of home computers, which are precisely the hope of American exponents of the 'computer democracy' idea? Soviet goals are linked with a fear of losing *political* control, whereas American goals have to do with *economic* profitability (not to mention control).

This is what we mean by 'technology is a human construction'. It is always geared to specific goals; shaped by the decisions of people in big business, governments, and organizations. It is naive to think of technological progress proceeding according to its own logic as if it were a 'thing' apart from people. Technology betrays its origins in particular societies and cultures. This is an arena of huge debate. There are two major questions:

● **Is technology neutral?** Those who believe so say that it is simply what is *done or not done* with technology which makes the difference. Thus the near disaster in the American nuclear power station at Three Mile Island, or the actual disaster at the Union Carbide chemical plant in Bhopal could be blamed on inadequate policies or inadequate technology. In this view, the application of technology to some process or problem is merely a technical task, undistorted by political or economic factors, or by human selfishness or greed.

Over against this, others insist that technology is never neutral. The University of California's Langdon Winner asks the question: 'Do artifacts have politics?', and proceeds to answer, 'Yes'.[6] Think of the bridges over the parkways in Long Island, New York. Why are they so low (sometimes only nine feet high at the kerb)? According to his biographer,

Robert Moses designed the bridges to allow whites (in their cars) but not blacks (who tended to ride in twelve-foot buses) to use the roads for recreation and commuting.

Of course, the 'neutral technologists' could claim this for their case: the bridge height should be raised. But what of the expense? Could one generate political will strong enough to alter this artifact?

Consider a further case. America's best-known historian and critic of technology, Lewis Mumford, points to two traditions of technology: authoritarian and democratic.[7] Many put nuclear power in the former category. That is, the very technology entails a high level of risk (of accident, terrorism, theft of plutonium, waste disposal and so on) which has to be contained by a strong state using extensive surveillance and policing. Does this artifact not have politics?

Such examples could naturally generate exasperation, especially among designers, sales staff or users of new technology. 'How could our "user-friendly" computers be anything but benign?' they might ask. 'It confuses the issue to drag in emotive examples such as lethal chemicals or nuclear waste.' Well, we shall see. Let me stress that I am not in any way wishing to deny or minimize either the beneficial applications of IT, or the good intentions of those involved in new technology as producers, salespeople or advisers.

By insisting that technology is a human construction we simply highlight the fact that *choices* are involved. And much hangs on those choices. For example, machine tool workers, who once used their skill and judgment in cutting metal to shape, now find their skills embodied in a computer, and thus not required. Decisions are made to 'deskill' these jobs. But it is not 'progress', 'economic necessity', or 'technological imperatives' which determine them. There is evidence, which we shall come to later, that people do not have to be subordinate to machines, losing their initiative or control to them. IT can be developed in alternative ways which are subject to human skill, and which co-operate with it.[8]

● **Does technology cause our problems?** In this view, technology has, as it were, a life of its own. It proceeds according to its own momentum, disregarding human welfare altogether. Once in place, the assembly line or computer system demands various back-up services, improved components, and so on until we are its lackeys. Eventually technology itself is feared as the enemy, the Frankenstein monster which overpowers its makers.

Jacques Ellul, a prominent French technology critic who works from a Christian standpoint, seems to come close to saying just this, that technology itself is evil. Two points should be noted here:

● Ellul is right to spotlight the self-perpetuating or self-augmenting character of technology.[9] Technology does seem to breed itself. In the case of computers, this is clear. Multitudes of little alterations made to machines as they are used in more and more diverse ways have the effect of making computers appear to 'evolve' almost on their own. (Who, a few years ago, would have thought of computers with 'mice' or 'joysticks' to enable their users to draw or play games?) Moreover, they are allowed to 'self-breed', without reference to external guidance, evaluation, or limits. Technology rules.

Or does it? Ellul's point about technology breeding technology is important, but incomplete. The 'interference' in the 'breeding' process is *economic*. It is hard to miss the fact that in today's information technology climate the temperature is raised by intense *competition*. The papers are full of stories about the crazy Christmas computer rush, the profits of British Telecom or Fujitsu, or dread fears about Sinclair or Apple, not to mention Silicon Valley itself. The precise connections are unclear, and a matter of debate.[10] But technology is patently more likely to develop in areas that *pay*.

● Ellul exposes another side to technology: its religious meaning. Writing before the advent of the microcomputer (which I think has helped to attract more people to this form of faith) Ellul says that 'the power of technique, mysterious though scientific, which covers the whole earth with its networks of waves, wires, and paper, is to the technician the abstract idol which gives him a reason for living and even for joy.'[11]

In both these ways, Ellul points to real dangers: technology treated as if it were a law to itself, and technology worshipped as an idol. Those who accept the self-breeding argument should pause to consider how in fact economic forces help shape technology. But the mistake of some who would thus correct Ellul is to see *only* economic forces at work, or to see them as the *basic* shapers of technology.[12] Ellul rescues us from this error by exposing another — one might say fundamental — layer of explanation, at the cultural or religious level.

Technology is a human construction, a human activity. Its basic ambiguity springs from this fact. The technological process is not in itself evil, nor in itself good. But nor is it neutral, beyond the reach of goodness or badness. Believing as I do that we inhabit a God-centred universe, I see that everything within that universe either affirms or denies a proper meaning and value — including human technological activity. The trouble is that the culture within which that activity takes place is misdirected. And the structures of industry, politics, and consumption, within which technology is embedded, are distorted. So, with our basic assumptions flawed, our technology is always in grave danger of being *mis*shaped. We all have a share in this misshaping process, when it occurs, colluding with and perpetuating it. But could the corollary also hold — that we can resist such misshaping, and craft alternatives to it? If indeed it is a human construction, why not?

Clearing the ground

How can we shape new technology before it shapes us? Or more to the point, how may we evaluate technological change? And how may we contribute to its proper shaping? My answer to these questions is firmly rooted in a Christian world-view. But before seeing where that takes us, let us clear the ground.

● The first obstacle is 'technofreaks and technophobes'. We are bombarded with wildly divergent opinions about new technology, opinions which are liable to influence our thinking. On the one hand is the bright and cheerful future: the sci-fi world of computer wizard Sir Clive Sinclair's robot slaves[13] or the 'communicative era' forecast by Professor Tom Stonier in which social problems will be microelectronically eliminated before they arise in real life.[14]

On the other hand is the future as seen by the pessimists: those who have just lost a whole chapter of the book they were writing or the accounts they were checking because they hit the wrong button by mistake; those who have received their seventh threatening letter from the tax-office computer, claiming they owe thousands; those who read Orwell at bedtime. If *this* is the age of information, they say, you can keep it! We must avoid simply slipping mindlessly into one of those camps.

● The second obstacle is the 'ethical vacuum'. Philosopher Hans Jonas has highlighted the desperate need for guidance in making the kinds of technological choices (or should we say economic, political, and social choices?) we have been discussing.[15] Few people have adjusted their ethics from the age of local communities and age-old tradition to our present-day realities of trans-national corporations and future orientation. Of course, future orientation has not been lacking in the past. It is our modern variety, with its planning mentality and its ability to interfere with the structure of the earth on which its existence depends, which is different, and thus demands a different ethical response.

Digging trenches in the street to lay cables for new telecommunications affects not only this generation, but the next. This illustrates the long-term aspect. Monitoring coffee crops in Kenya, using remote sensing devices in satellites, affects not just one country, but several. Such information may not be available to Kenyans themselves, if they cannot afford the computers and satellites involved. This illustrates the global aspect. On a scale never known before, says Jonas, technological decisions are *long-term* and *global* ones.

Jonas sees deep irony here. Just when modern technological development is so potent a force for human survival or annihilation, the same drives that stimulate technology have helped deflect attention from the very wisdom which might avert disaster. Our technological exploits — humans in space, test-tube babies — reinforce our belief that we can get along without outside assistance. An impetus once crucial to early science and technology — namely to serve God by understanding and harnessing the natural world — has been drained away. Now we pursue technology for its own sake, and even believe it has its own logic.

● The third obstacle is the 'Lynn White syndrome'. Christianity has been blamed for some of the blights of modern technology. So how could it possibly provide guidance now? Lynn White's famous paper 'The historic roots of our ecologic crisis' focussed this accusation.[16] Its main thrust is that the Jewish-Christian claim to superiority over nature removed the final obstacle to its exploitation. When thought of as 'sacred', creation could be protected. Without that shield, the rape of the earth could begin.

Let no Christian evade the charge that some have failed to keep their technological activity in step with their faith (and sadly, still do). Nor have Christians helped remove the impression that having dominion over nature means dominating rather than co-operating with nature in our stewardship. Moreover, our record of reflection on the ethics of technology *is* rather thin, though there are signs of this changing today.[17]

Where White misleads is in his almost total failure to report the contribution of the Renaissance to the rise of modern technology. For by taking God out of the picture, the dualism, yes even the conflict, between humans and nature is sharpened. Without any check on self-directed human activity, the destructive *hubris* of modern technology began in earnest. This can be seen in Francis Bacon. Though still using Christian words, the sentiment is decisively that of the Renaissance. Technology, for Bacon, will one day cure the effects of the human fall from grace.

Having cleared the ground, then, how should we use this space?

Agenda for action
My message is: don't accept technology as 'given' or 'inevitable'. Explore its roots. Shape its fruits. Let me suggest

three things to bear in mind as we try to shape technology for a human world: responsibility, idolatry, and hope. These guidelines for our agenda derive directly from the biblical outlook already mentioned.

● **Accept responsibility**. In a biblical perspective, the creation story yields the basic technological charter. Humans are entrusted with the task of caring for the earth and opening up its potential for the good of all. Within the creation, humans have the unique possibility of communicating with God. We are, literally, *answerable* for the way we live.

Within the broad context of 'stewardship' of the earth's resources, our specific responsibility in technology is in the everyday world of human relationships. For as technology is about the way we *do* things, a human construction, questions of power, justice, and the quality of social relationships are paramount. Think of the Old Testament stress on care in building technology (no flat-roof buildings without safety parapets), and on agriculture geared to the needs of *all society*, including the very poor. Think also of the husbanding of *human* resources. Jesus' parable about the 'talents' is surely more about *relationships*, about trust, than about money.

The impact of these issues is huge. They broaden the scope of today's technological discussions. For the acceptance of responsibility means asking 'What is it *for*?' (Why is this computer system being installed — to enhance and work with the skills of the operator, or to move initiative and control to the office?), 'Who decides?' (Should the 'consumers of cable television have any part in choosing what sort of system is installed, given the difference it is likely to make in the long term?), 'Why are we doing this?' (Is 'if we don't develop superchips the Japanese will' a good enough reason for re-channelling technology?).

Today's climate is hostile to the idea of regulating technology. Even new technology agreements, and safeguards relating to health and safety, for instance of glare from visual display units, are fairly undeveloped. Data protection in Britain is, frankly, feeble. But I wish to suggest that more, not less of these areas should be explored, each in an appropriate context.

Christian practice sits uneasily alongside both capitalist and state socialist ideologies. We cannot endorse either a society based on individualism or one in which the state, the party, or the society as a whole is the focus of attention. As Michael Schluter of the Jubilee Centre in Cambridge says, the alternative is to work towards a proper *quality* of relationships.[18] He points out that the thrust of biblical social teaching emphasizes the place of *love*, and asks how this can be built into our social arrangements — families, firms, government, and so on.

We must develop information technology in ways which enhance the quality of human relationships. Of course, this might *sound* like what some IT optimists say, that IT will bring about a decentralized, home-centred, caring society, with user-friendly machines in the electronic cottage. But technology itself cannot produce such effects. It is a human construction. Which is why, if any of those nice-sounding dreams are to be realized, questions of 'what is it for?', 'who decides?' and 'what is the right way forward?' must persistently be asked. Wider questions of justice and power must also be faced if the quality of human relationships is to be fostered by IT.

● **We should expect idolatry.** The deliberate rejection of God from human life does not mean that people no longer have any object of devotion, reverence or service. Desperately trying to escape the effects of this rebellion Cain builds a city. Later, and on a larger scale, the story of Babel recounts how technological independence and self-sufficiency were embodied in a notorious tower. Is IT not treated today as if it could become the saviour, at least of Western economies? Did I hear someone say that Silicon Valley holds the keys to the kingdom?

Oxford computer scientist, Michael Shallis, has also observed this phenomenon — the worship of new technology — and describes it in his book, *The Silicon Idol*.[19] Dirk Hanson, who wrote *The New Alchemists* (about Silicon Valley),[20] sees a new 'priesthood' developing among computer whiz-kids and technofreaks. Others, without Christian convictions, see the same thing: a new form of idolatry.

The significance of this should not be missed. It relates to questions we have already asked: 'what is going on here?', 'what are the underlying motives?' New technology is no more religiously neutral than it is politically neutral. It relates to themes already mentioned: Jacques Ellul's critique of the power and attraction of technology today. No wonder people *fear* as well as stand in awe of new technology. No wonder people believe that only more technology can solve our problems, including those they see as technologically generated. Idols bind us and blind us.

● **We must live in hope.** This stands in stark contrast with what I have just said. But intentionally so. Like rainbow light against a dark threatening sky, the Christian message is bursting with hope. Ask yourself, 'what is my underlying attitude to new technology, and what is it based on?' Dutch engineer (and now politician) Egbert Schuurman says that the Christian meaning of technology includes 'emancipating the body and mind from toil and drudgery, repelling the onslaughts of nature, providing for man's material needs, and conquering diseases . . . eliminating unnecessary burdens, freeing time, promoting rest and peace . . .'[21]

Let us exchange high-tech hype for high-tech hope, hope vested in the potential offered by the responsible development of technology. This draws us to God rather than to technology itself. Where is the basis for technology yoked to the quality of human relationships? 'Greater love has no one than this,' said Jesus, 'that he lay down his life for his friends.' Acceptance of that love provides the fresh start and the needed dynamic.

Look out for signs of hope. Perhaps Schuurman is in the Dutch parliament for 'such a time as this'? There are others like him in influential positions in government and big companies. Some new technology agreements *do* promise to retain the skills of workers when computerization takes place. Some high-tech establishments refuse certain kinds of project — the Warwick Science Park, for instance, does no work on fission-fusion in weapons research and no work involving live animal experiments. Such self-limitations deserve to be more widely tried. Some IT firms do have a policy of putting people before profit. There are signs of hope. We must not forget them.

What, then, is the 'silicon scenario'? Is it a society based on hope in technological salvation? If so, then its future is shaky, like a house built on sand (from which silicon derives). The alternative is to find appropriate guidelines and practices for shaping new technology in non-idolatrous ways. In other words, to build on rock. This, as Jesus said, means hearing his words, *and doing them*.

Notes

1 Quoted in Dirk Hanson, *The New Alchemists: Silicon Valley and the Microelectronics Revolution*, Little, Brown and Co., 1982, pages 12, 16

2 Shirley Williams, *A Job to Live: The Impact of New Technology on Society*, Penguin, 1985

3 Barry Jones, *Sleepers Awake! New Technology and the Future of Work*, Wheatsheaf, 1982

4 Science Council of Canada, *Planning Now for an Information Society: Tomorrow Is Too Late*, Science Council, 1982

5 *The New York Times*, 20 May 1984, quoted in Elia Zureik, 'The Electronic Cottage: New Wine in Old Bottles?' Paper given at conference on 'Technology and Culture: Computers, Values, Creativity', University of Ottawa, May 1985

6 Langdon Winner, 'Do artifacts have politics?', in Donald MacKenzie and Judith Wacjman (eds) *The social shaping of technology*, Open University Press, 1985

7 Lewis Mumford, 'Authoritarian and democratic technics', *Technology and Culture*, 1964, pages 5, 1−8

8 Council for Science and Society, *New Technology, Employment, and Skill*, CSS, 1981, page 96

9 Ellul's term *la technique* embraces far more than mere machines or artifacts. It includes any way of doing things for a purpose. See Jacques Ellul, *The Technological Society*, London: Cape, 1964; New York: Vintage

10 Some economists doubt whether people really do make 'rational economic choices' in the way that classical economics supposes. See Jon Elster, *Explaining Technical Change*, Cambridge University Press, 1983. But this does not affect the drift of my argument, which is that technology is shaped not only by its own momentum, but also by economic choices.

11 Ellul (see above), page 144

12 Some Marxist critiques of technology have this character. Accepting the force of some Marxian arguments and analysis certainly does not entail acceptance of a complete 'Marxist package'. See David Lyon, 'Marxist misgivings about information technology' in Agit Jain and Alexandr Matejko (eds) *A Critique of Marxist and Non-Marxist Thought*, Praeger

13 Clive Sinclair, 'Robot future will be out of this world', *Practical Robotics*, July/August 1984, pages 61–62

14 Tom Stonier, *The Wealth of Information*, Thames and Hudson, 1983

15 Hans Jonas, *The Imperative of Responsibility*, Oxford University Press, 1984

16 Lynn White, 'The historic roots of our ecologic crisis', *Science*, 1970, CLV, 3707, 1203–1207. See also Colin Russell, *Cross Currents*, Inter-Varsity Press, 1985

17 Egbert Schuurman, *Technology and the Future*, Wedge, 1980; Robin Attfield, *The Ethics of Environmental Concern*, Oxford University Press, 1983

18 Roy Clements and Michael Schluter, *Reconstructing the Extended Family*, Jubilee, 1985

19 Michael Shallis, *The Silicon Idol*, Oxford University Press, 1984

20 Dirk Hanson (see above)

21 Egbert Schuurman, *Reflections on the Technological Society*, Wedge, 1977, page 21

2
Automation, jobs and work

When the 200-year-old Courage brewery business opened a high-tech lager plant in Berkshire, England, many former employees were so anxious about what they saw there that they opted for redundancy or early retirement. Gone were the old 'coppers', in which wort is boiled vigorously; they were replaced by gleaming stainless steel. Gone was the old pace of work. Now high-speed production and canning is controlled from a central computer console which automatically dispatches in the correct sequence the right quantities of the ingredients required for a particular brew. No wonder workers were dizzied by the prospect of shifting to a shiny, automated workplace.

However, many did make the move. Unions and management alike regarded the whole operation as a success — with a few qualifications. Two aims were kept in the forefront when decisions were made: for the brewery to make a profit and be competitive in relation to stringent production requirements, and for high standards of working conditions, relationships and personnel policies, alongside good amenities and environment. New machinery was not installed at the expense of workers. Rather, as much decision-making as possible was retained within each redesigned job. Much routine and repetitive work was removed by automation, but the production process remains firmly under human control. The relatively smooth transition to the new high-tech site has been put down to the deliberate involvement of all in the process of change, and commitment to quality of working-life principles.[1]

So what difference will information technology make to jobs and work? The Berkshire brewery shows us both sides of the new technology coin: anxiety and job-loss on the one hand, and the opportunity for flexibility and the development of new skills on the other. New technology always inspires both technofreaks and technophobes. Today sees a new rash of each genre. Which is appropriate for IT?

It was Czech playwright Karel Capek who gave us the word 'robot'. In his play, *RUR* (1921), robots turned against their human creators in a robot revolution. This common literary theme echoes the fears of many ordinary people. Will machines eventually get the better of us? Will our special skills and our means of making a living be snatched from us by metal claws? Will the reign of the robots begin?

Listen also to the other voice, heard in novels, films, and on television. It tells a futurist tale of a Cockaigne-like land of peace and plenty. (You haven't heard of Cockaigne? It was a medieval fantasy land where larks flew ready-cooked into the mouths of the peasants.) In this utopia automated machines take the toil and drudgery out of life, leaving a leisured society in their place. The 'robot valet' and the 'rock-a-bye robot' take over domestic labours while the automated factory and office drastically reduce 'human factor' requirements in the world of production and commerce.

What is happening in the real world? Do we have a warrant either to issue dire warnings or to hold out rosy promises? The actual context of the push towards IT is the international scramble to climb out of the recession of the 1980s. Economies are rapidly restructuring. Politicians, industrialists, and labour unions try to repair what now appears as the mismatch of jobs and skills. The Japanese 'fifth generation' threat has galvanized other advanced societies into feverish activity.

The impact of IT must be considered in the light of these factors, plus others: the already high unemployment levels, to which some believed we would never return after the inter-war depression; the already existing disparities between depressed, 'sunset industry' regions such as Detroit or Merseyside, and their 'sunrise' opposites, such as Denver or Milton Keynes; and the growing gaps between nations in the Northern and Southern hemispheres.

With the trend towards automation of both factory and

office, what is the prospect for jobs and the quality of working life? Does IT spell 'automatic unemployment', or will new 'service industry' — or for that matter manufacturing — jobs open up as IT expands? Beyond this, to examine the impact of IT is to raise basic questions about the meaning and purpose of work. Such questions have been traditionally answered in terms of the so-called 'Protestant ethic'. Is this ethic now outdated? Should it be replaced? Or is ancient wisdom about work — in particular the affirmation that work is close to the heart of humanness — still relevant to the 'information age'? If we are to shape tomorrow's technology, rather than just allowing ourselves to be shaped by it, then some way of wisdom to direct our efforts must be found. But not only 'found'. It must be translated into practical proposals.

Steel collar workers?

'Less room for human error' proclaimed the Fiat car billboard, but 'More room for humans'. This is the explanation: these cars are 'handbuilt by robots'. 'Steel collar workers' have joined the labour force. The silicon chip holds out the promise of automated production. From design board to delivery schedule, the computer makes a huge difference to traditional ways of making things. This also means big changes for people. Does automation eliminate jobs and skills? Or does it create new ones?

Do you remember Charlie Chaplin's flailing arms and flying wrench as he tried in vain to keep pace with the passing conveyor belt in *Modern Times*? The assembly line became the symbol of mechanized production in the twentieth century. But it was only one more stage in the process of using machines to aid human work which has been going on since the beginning of industrialism.

By the 1950s, with the arrival of the first computers, thoughts began to turn towards the complete automation of the workplace — fictionally represented in Kurt Vonnegut's book, *Player Piano*. The pianola 'plays itself' as tape is fed in, and thus reflects the reality of the factory down the road where computer punch cards keep the production line going. Vonnegut's vision of the society, split between the technical elite on the one hand, and the aimless and superfluous mass on the other, makes sobering reading.

The arrival of cheap integrated circuits in the late 1970s made possible an accelerating trend towards automated production. The new chips could co-ordinate complex production processes and increase the efficiency and accuracy of machines. If machinery once enhanced brawn power, new computers enhance brain power.

Automation takes place in different ways:

● In process industries such as oil refineries, chemical plants, and power generation, raw materials are transformed in an ongoing flow, in which maintaining constant conditions such as temperature and pressure is vital. Microchip technology makes possible more complete integration and control of such processes. The measuring instruments are themselves computerized, and feed their signals into a central computer, programmed to monitor the whole process. Few jobs are lost in such industries, because they are already highly automated. The Berkshire brewery is a relevant example.

● Micro-electronic devices may be built into individual machines. Metal-cutting or wood-turning, which once depended on the subjective judgment of the craftsman, may now be controlled by computer. Cutters, grinders, and drillers have been computerized for a long time — but only for simple and repetitive tasks. The new chip-controlled machines are far more versatile and flexible, because they can so easily be reprogrammed for different jobs. A computer-numerically-controlled machine tool, for instance, can be programmed to cut and shape metal according to precise specifications, even for a small batch.

Here, the social and personal impact is far greater, especially the risk of deskilling. In this context 'deskilling' is the term used to describe what happens to a person's job when his or her skills are 'taught' to a computer, which then does the job, or part of it, by itself. The engineer in the office takes over what used to be a shop-floor responsibility and skill. On a larger scale, deskilling means that fewer and fewer skilled people are required to operate machines. As we shall see, computer-controlled machines do not *necessarily* deskill. There are alternatives.

Another development, as machines are computerized, is that workers are offered alternative jobs. This happened at the Japanese newspaper *Asahi Shimbun* where the skills of middle-aged print-workers were transferred to computers. They were obliged to take unskilled jobs as security guards or salesmen.[2] In this case, no role was left for the people who had previously been print-workers. New technology and new organization made their skills redundant. At the same time, there is a rising skills level in some sectors of the work-force. Some fear that this could lead to a 'Player Piano' society polarized between those with and those without qualifications, skills and jobs.

● The third type of automation involves robots. Not the human-like androids of *Star Wars* fame, or even the older raspy-voiced daleks from *Dr Who*. These robots are programmable machines most frequently used to spray paint, to weld, and do other unpleasant or hazardous tasks. Japan easily leads the world in their production and use. As they become more sophisticated, and are enabled to 'see' and 'feel' — developments already well under way — they will be a proportionately greater threat to jobs. At present — though this is changing — people are often still required to check that the component is actually there to be sprayed or welded by the robot!

Robots will be 'job-killers' in the long term. One of the most striking forecasts, from Carnegie-Mellon University, says that over the next twenty years, 3 out of 8 million manufacturing jobs in the USA could be taken over by robots. By 2025, nearly all manufacturing chores will be done by robots.[3] (Similar dire forecasts of twenty years ago have not in fact come true. The evidence suggests much slower change is likely.) Although their installation is relatively slow now the pace may quicken as costs fall. Shirley Williams points out that an 'arc-welding robot can now be bought for about twice the annual wage of a skilled man'. Unlike him, the robot can work almost continuously, bringing an annual return on outlay of up to three times higher than the human equivalent.[4]

Apart from commercial criteria, people often justify installing robots by pointing out the dirty or dangerous nature of jobs replaced. But other factors are also present. People may still have to do risky or repetitive work bringing materials to robots. They may feel isolated or more machine-paced if their neighbours have been replaced by robots. Discussing *Dallas* is not the same any more!

Automated factory visionaries entertain hopes that one day the currently piecemeal adoption of automated technique will be joined together in a so-called 'flexible manufacturing system'. As in the story of the automated factory, with only a man and a dog on the shop floor. The man has to feed the dog. The dog has to ensure the man doesn't touch the machinery. Computer-aided design of final products and components would be used to decide on the ideal plant for production. A central computer would co-ordinate the activities of all individual computerized machines which contribute to the operation and final product. That in turn would be scrutinized by computerized quality control. Few contemporary manufacturers seem close to realizing this dream, at least in its fullest dimensions.

Nevertheless, aspects of the dream are already with us. Computer-aided design and manufacture means that parts may be drawn and transferred to the shop-floor electronically. The designer's job is made far easier by instantly being able to see the part in its different dimensions, or in association with others. But it can mean a loss of *social* relationships, as he or she no longer has to visit the shop-floor in person to discuss the design with the machinist.[5] New technology always seems to present two faces!

Let me be candid. We simply do not know the answers to many important questions about the effects of IT on jobs and work in production. It is still too early to say with any confidence to what extent unemployment will be alleviated or worsened by automation. In some instances, such as the new computerized signalling system on the magnificently scenic

Dingwall to Kyle railway line in Scotland, labour, and its cost, is simply eliminated in the quest to make the line less uneconomic. But in others, such as some fourteen German firms which introduced new technology (CAD), a net increase in jobs was reported.[6]

Nor do we know in any detail what will happen to traditional skills involved in work, as computers are increasingly 'taught' to do what people once did. Some people are made to feel worthless as machines take over their jobs. Others face new challenges as their jobs require more skill because computerized machines are involved.

The fact that we do not know details is no excuse for assuming that things will eventually work out for the best — which is often the attitude of new technology pioneers. They assure us that, short term, few jobs will be lost because the transition will not take place overnight. They warn that the real danger is hesitating to adopt new technology, and defending existing (but doomed) practices. But this is only half the story.

We do know that the kinds of jobs available change as new technology is introduced (often more skilled, and fewer unskilled jobs) which means that the costs of change fall on those who cannot find employment. We do know that the chip simultaneously affects diverse areas, including those which were once looked to as sponges to soak up laid-off labour. And we do know that the dominant trend in automation thus far has been deskilling. Although exceptions exist to all these rules (and in some cases we simply do not have adequate information), to ignore them is to evade responsibility in technological change.

We may not pretend that the issues are in any way cut-and-dried. But what we already see happening ought to give us pause for thought. We accept that IT brings tremendous benefits in terms of raised productivity, flexibility, and so on. But we should also prepare ourselves for the kinds of problems that arise in the wake of IT. For technology is a *human* construction. It is something *we do*, and it is shaped by the decisions of managers and unions (as well as governments, universities, and others). To say we do not know the future, and even to put our money on IT industries as the best hope, is to deny responsibility *now*. In a world where productivity tends to be put before people we desperately need guidance about appropriate ways to develop and install new technology.

Towards an electronic office?

The headlines say it all: 'The man who has given up paper.' 'Are secretaries an endangered species?' 'Smooth way to the automatic office.' But what do they mean?

The man who gave up paper in this particular story is Tom Rosewall, an executive with Westinghouse Furniture Systems. His 'paperless office' trick is done with 'electronic mail'. He simply dials British Telecom's electronic mail computer, Telecom Gold, types in the letter, which then arrives in seconds at his colleague's desk in Hong Kong or Highgate. If his colleague is in the USA, he or she is one of more than 2.5 million electronic mail users.[7]

This is one angle on the office of the future. It concerns the coupling of traditional office communications with new technology. The main result is fuller and faster communications than were possible using telephone and telex. But it also means that people who previously had to work in close proximity can now be dispersed around the globe, in a 'network' across the city or, more mundanely, around the suburbs.

But what of the secretary as an endangered species? Here is the other angle on the 'office of the future', the automation of clerical work. One morning the boss announces that the typewriter and notepad are going, and that a word processor is to be installed in their place. Some typists are delighted to find that their mistakes will no longer be detected by the tell-tale white correcting fluid, or that when the boss wants a line altered right in the middle of a document they don't have to retype the whole thing. Others say it takes away their secretarial role. One London secretary said: 'At the end of the day you feel, when you've switched off the machine, that you've unplugged yourself.'[8] Yet others live in dread of the day when the voice-recognizing machine prints out their letters of notice.

Because the idea of an automated factory has been around for some time (though not in relation to microcomputers), it is perhaps easier to grasp than the idea of an automated office. Yet the trends and impacts of new office technologies may well be more dramatic than those of production, not least because they are occurring at the same time as the chip hits the factory.

Office and clerical work have been transformed over the past 100 years. The Dickensian male clerk, bent over his high desk with quill pen and unwieldy ledgers in a dusty, dingy, and cluttered room is gone for ever. In his place is the modern, usually female, manipulator of typewriter, telephone and photocopier, now attempting to adjust to the word processor, within an artificially-lit, softly-partitioned open-plan room. Other significant differences are that there is now a vast army of clerical workers (around thirty per cent of the work-force), and that whereas the male clerk laboured in hope of promotion to management, his contemporary female counterpart is likely to have a much lowlier career path.

Although office 'information processing' was done at first with paper, pen and ink, files and cabinets, and using messengers and the mail, the twentieth century has seen big changes. The typewriter and telephone, the photocopier and telex mean more and more data is handled. As things change, offices need more capital equipment and fewer people.[9] Why do people mechanize and automate the office? To save costs, raise productivity, and also to keep up with the Joneses.[10]

The chip makes a tremendous impact in the office. But the secretary will be endangered as a species well before the paperless office arrives. It is cheaper to install word processors than complete information systems. Because the recession makes it hard to find capital, only the bigger organizations such as banks and insurance companies can afford full computerization. Beyond this, information systems themselves will have to improve a lot before they are acceptable as alternatives to time-tested methods. What are the main changes we can expect?

● First, improved office efficiency. Bureaucracy could become less cumbersome; decision-making better informed. Forecasts and alternative options are more quickly available in digestible form using computers. In jobs-and-work terms, this may mean the decline of the middle manager. These are people who, like personnel officers, gather together, compile and present data to their superiors. These jobs, which stand between basic information and the decision-makers, could be at risk. Some evidence suggests that secretaries, the initial handlers of information, could acquire some of these tasks as they become computer-literate.[11]

At the same time we must admit that this may be a disaster area. The actual performance of some machines does not seem to match the promises in the glossy advertisements. Because of the prestige involved in computerization, some make reckless purchases before ever obtaining advice about what the computer can actually do for them. Offices everywhere are strewn with unusable machines, gathering cobwebs. Less paper may well be used as electronic mail catches on. But a friend of mine who works for one of the world's biggest accountancy firms discovered on testing her 'Mac' that she used reams more paper than ever before, producing graphs, figures, and tables!

● The second, and more significant impact of IT in the office is the automation of clerical work. Many routine, low-paid administrative tasks done by women will be axed. Some jobs, using new telecommunications, will be done at home, thus reducing downtown office overheads. Whether in the office or the home, the jobs that remain could be subject to new strains. Physically, users of VDUs (visual display units — the screens) experience glare, leading to sore eyes, plus other physical discomforts, though not, we trust, terminal illness. (These side-effects are discussed by unions, and legislation, already available in Scandinavia, is being sought in Britain.[12])

Socially, signs of new strains are appearing. Bradford Council in West Yorkshire installed word processors early on (1977). They reduced staff at the Jacob's Well office by half, using nine machines, increased productivity by nineteen per cent, and saved £58–59,000 per year. But, as one secretary pointed out: 'The machines are in constant operation, and are programmed by the rate material comes in. The workers have one ten-minute break in the morning and afternoon, and otherwise have no contact with other workers during office time . . . The operator has almost no contact with the finished product . . .'[13] People using word processors tend to work more on their own, more intensively, and more under the boss's scrutiny.

All this may sound rather negative and pessimistic. Of course many secretaries take to word processors like ducks to water, and welcome them as wonderful weapons against drudgery. So what makes the difference? Let me suggest that their popularity relates directly to the *context* within which they are introduced.

Wang word processor advertisements state that their products 'require minimum operator training for maximum productivity'. Wang add that word processors 'give all that a good supervisor would know — only electronically. You couldn't fail to get to work on time.'[14] If a word processor is installed in the hope of tighter control of workers, no one need show surprise that the machine is negatively received. The same ambiguity in attitudes to new technology is markedly visible in the case of 'telecommuting'.

Could IT liberate us for ever from breathless commuting, urban congestion, and from the pollutive and wasteful use of oil fuels? An enticing thought! 'Telecommuting' offers all this and more. By working from home, using computer terminals wired up to others, some Americans believe they will save 750 million gallons of petrol. Right now, 'computer-ready' houses are available in Bencia, north of San Francisco. They have prewired dual phone lines and built-in computer furniture. The cost of the actual computer hardware is added to the mortgage.[15]

Many people enjoy the flexibility that homeworking brings, and there is evidence that some employers have seen productivity rise among telecommuters. In a survey of ten European countries, over a third of respondents said they would prefer to work at home.[16] And apart from the environmental benefits of decentralization, some, such as Toffler, say that telecommuting will contribute to a closer community spirit as the 'bedroom suburbs' come to life in the daytime. No one who observes with despair the way in which modern practices of commuting — indeed the general separation of home from work — has contributed to family tensions and community breakdown would be sorry to see a reversal of that trend. The potential for decentralization offered by IT deserves careful exploration.

But there is, as ever, a darker side. Although fashion designers, television producers or academics, sitting in their living rooms, may happily be creative and retain control of their flexitime work, prospects are quite different for others. Homeworking, which is particularly attractive for women with young children, already has some features of older homeworking situations: low pay, no security, isolation, and closer monitoring by the boss. Counting keystrokes of homeworkers is an employers' device which is on the increase. The latter, naturally enough, want to be sure that something productive is actually happening behind the domestic front door. But the worker soon finds that her keystroke figures have been analyzed by sophisticated software in a quest for improved performance.

Once more then, we discover that the changes made by the introduction of IT call for a sea change in attitudes and approaches. As with robotics in manufacturing, phenomena such as telecommuting are already taking place. But remember, the new technologies are not 'neutral'. They are humanly shaped from the start for good or ill. They are already with us, though it is not too late to encourage their responsible shaping, and resist the alternative. We badly need guidance which refers to more than commercial criteria or hype-dreams. For it is not some narrow segment of paid employment we are discussing. We are confronted with potential transformations of life as we know it.

More of the same?

The Japan Robot Leasing Company rents robots to people

who want to bring IT into their garden sheds. This means that simple toys can be turned out, or hi-fi equipment spray-painted without massive capital expense. Small businesses find computerized production within their grasp. At my college, our department secretary is delighted with what her word processor has meant to her work. Both storing academic records and producing the day-to-day memos and course descriptions is far more efficient.

New technology holds out great promise for the world of work. Much drudgery, routine and unpleasant toil may be taken over by computerized machines. We have cause to be grateful for the silicon chip. And nothing critical I say should minimize that gratitude. But as new technology is always devised and developed in an ambiguous and far from perfect world, it will always appear as a mixed blessing.

The overwhelming reason given for installing robots is to reduce labour costs. (The situation is different with computer-numerical-controlled machine tools, where the primary aim does not seem to be dispensing with skilled labour.) In human terms, 'reducing labour requirements' all too often means striking a blow at people's self-esteem, and adding to the lines of those whose talents and energies are simply rotting. And for those who still have jobs, new technology may well mean a less skilled task, or alienation, as with the typist who felt she'd 'unplugged herself' at the end of the day. But why is this? Surely mass unemployment and alienation were features of the passing 'industrial society', not of the chip-based 'information society'?

The big danger when we talk of 'transformations of human life' is to imagine that *everything* is changing. But is it? Although many things we take for granted may change (such as single careers, or working away from home), in other ways it is 'business as usual'. The pursuit of continued economic growth, the desire to compete for profits and market shares, the challenge of technological mastery continue.

None of these may be wrong or misguided in itself. But we must be realistic. 'Silicon idolatry' also lives on, blinding us to the interests and purposes really being served, and deflecting our attention from issues which should be far higher on our agenda. We have seen how IT often brings 'more of the same' as far as work is concerned: isolation, machine-pacing, initiative and responsibility passed from shop-floor to office.

At the same time, we must quickly ask, does the silicon (or any other) idol have us totally in its grasp? If the answer is 'no', then we may also affirm the rightness of a creative quest for technological development, appropriately and responsibly sought. And we should also look for signs of hope which indicate that the future does not have to be 'more of the same'.

We have looked at changes in the nature of jobs and in work situations. The other key issue is employment. Are the optimists right? Trusting market mechanisms, or 'long waves' of economic activity,[17] the optimists believe that in the long haul jobs lost through labour-saving devices will be recovered in new fields. It has happened before, they say: 2 million Britons moved from manufacturing to services (education, health, entertainment and so on) between 1961 and 1981. We cannot predict exactly how, any more than early car makers could foresee the jobs created around sales and service. But it can happen again.

Or are the pessimists right? Clive Jenkins and Barrie Sherman dramatically predict the 'collapse of work'.[18] They warn that it is nonsense to expect jobs to arise, phoenix-like, from the ruins of industrial society. What chance is there of workers displaced by robots finding new jobs in the 'service sector' when that sector, too, is being automated?

Information technology is thus right at the heart of one of the most pressing problems of the late twentieth century. But do not blame the chip! And do not listen to those who imply that failure to acquire the 'right skills' inflates statistics of the jobless. Scapegoats are too easily found! The world-wide recession is the primary cause.

The backdrop to the chip's arrival, however, is rather sombre and, in fact, affects how we view the chip. The University of Warwick's Employment Institute sees only about 150,000 new jobs being created in the UK up to 1990. Just over 1 million full-time jobs will go, and nearly as many part-time jobs will appear. Self-employment will rise, but manufacturing industry is expected to shed another 500,000 workers. The picture in other advanced nations is similar.

Will the growth of high-tech industry make a difference? In the USA, where both the labour market and people have been more flexible, the shift to new industries has been more rapid than in Europe. But if their evidence is anything to go by, IT job-creation is not a great hope. By 1995 no more than 4 per cent of non-agricultural workers will be in high-tech industries. They tend to automate their own production lines. By 1985 even Silicon Valley was heavy with gloom. Plant closures and lay-offs led the papers to ask whether the boom had already ended.

Although there is little call for complacency, the overall picture is not one of unmitigated doom. Fears of massive 'automatic unemployment' have not been realized. There is a growing demand (in a limited area) for *more* labour of the skilled and technical variety. Let us talk of the 'restructuring' rather than the 'destruction' of formal employment. Still, this does take its toll.

Wastage of human energies has already been mentioned. With regard to IT, two other factors are crucial. One is regional disparities. When new jobs do appear, they are not in areas of highest joblessness. The 'green field' or 'sunbelt' sites, not the inner city, see employment growth. The other factor is that particular groups carry the costs of change. Young people, those deemed 'too old' to start again, ethnic minorities, and women all suffer. (Even the high-tech scientists have to watch for their jobs if they reach the grand age of thirty-five — Phillips Electronics in Surrey are looking for volunteers in this age bracket to move to less demanding jobs.)

Clearly, old theories have to be revised. History won't conveniently repeat itself so that we know what to expect. But perhaps IT can help us? Jonathan Gershuny says we ought not to dismiss too readily the idea that 'services' could create new jobs. Not so much 'garage' or 'health' servicing, but 'self-servicing', based on IT.

Shopping from home, remote learning (as in the British Open University), or even remote diagnosis would be examples of 'self-servicing'. They depend on producing more hard- and soft-ware, and could thus help stimulate the creation of jobs providing not final services but the where-withal for self-servicing.[19] Gershuny's speculations are based in part on already-established trends towards more work being done in the 'informal economy', so it could possibly become a 'sign of hope'. But even this cannot bring much joy to the *unskilled* unemployed. Big questions remain.

Whatever approach is preferred, we must stress that things will not improve by themselves. To hold out hope of economic recovery is one thing. To show care for those affected by restructuring *now* is another.

The Swedish experience has lessons for us here. Sweden, one of the most highly computerized societies in the world, has successfully established process control systems, industrial robots, air traffic control systems, and office terminals. But the Swedes have also taken great care to consider the social and human effects of new technology, and to ensure that the maximum number of people have a say in its development.

Cambridge industrial relations researcher, Colin Gill, has studied the Scandinavian style in depth. He believes that their high level of awareness of what new machines mean to *people* as well as just what machines can *do* sets a pattern worth following. With will, a degree of consensus, and decision-making at all levels, there is an alternative to simply letting things happen.[20]

The question still remains. Why should we go one direction rather than another? Remembering that investment in IT has *long-term* consequences, what should guide our choices about employment and working conditions? Can we offer any alternative to the accepted wisdom of the day?

A redundant work ethic?

Do we have any new insights on IT, work, and employment? This question forces us to re-examine the work ethic — still the main source of conventional wisdom on the matter in the

West. Our confusion about it is picked up nicely in a cartoon I have at home. A dishevelled businessman shrugs despairingly. The caption reads: 'Oh boy! When I have to stay late at the office it's "workaholic!''. When I don't want to mow the lawn it's "where's your Protestant work ethic?" '

Protestantism is said to be closely connected with the birth of the modern world. Indeed, modern science and technology along with capitalism and industrialism all owe some of their early impetus to Protestant Christian practice.

But today the 'Protestant work ethic' is under attack. Who needs a work ethic? The prosperous and playful member of the 'leisure society', which is based on the 'wealth of information'? The depressed and demoralized worker who ten years ago lost his job to a robot? The advent of the silicon chip has served to underline this question. In a world where 'work' is of diminishing significance, who needs a work ethic? This question demands an answer at several levels.

● **Was the 'work ethic' once relevant but now redundant?** As this is not the main focus of my book I shall short-circuit the debate, coming straight to the point. Since Puritan times, the work ethic has become encrusted with unchristian accretions. The idea that success in work is evidence of God's blessing (fair enough in itself) was gradually stretched to include the converse: that failure means non-acceptance with God. And when God was quietly dropped from the picture, work came to equal worth.

So far, so bad. But things got worse. For with the rise of industry, organized under capitalist principles, *paid employment* became the main means of earning a living. 'Work as worth' became 'paid employment as worth'. Having a job was associatcd (and still is) with fulfilling a moral duty. Why else, when the evidence so clearly points in the opposite direction, are unemployed people still suspected of laziness or welfare scrounging?[21]

The Reformers and their Puritan followers *did* stress the value of work. William Tyndale, for instance, would not have recognized today's devaluing of domestic labour: 'There is no better work than to please God, to pour water, to wash dishes, to be a souter (cobbler) or an apostle is all one . . .'[22] Luther shared the same view. Work is a means of fulfilling our humanity. Calvin, using the same biblical sources, brought out the importance of *useful* work, plus the value of human interdependence and solidarity fostered by working co-operatively with others. Biblically, then, work is a 'labour of love'.

The curse on work, which followed human estrangement from God, twisted what was initially good, self-fulfilling, and even a way of 'worship'. It also meant that some people had to be *persuaded* to work. Not everyone shared the old Protestant ideals. Indeed, historically as well as now, most regard the job as a necessary evil. But Victorian industrialists often *used* those ideals as a means of persuasion. Today, Japanese-style commitment to corporate goals is recommended as another tool of persuasion.

The Renaissance may partly be blamed for the elevation of work to the centre of human existence. This mistake was rein-forced by Marx and his friends. Though they correctly diag-nosed some of the ills of labour within capitalism, they remained trapped in the belief that to liberate labour is to liberate humanity. Paradoxically (as Krishan Kumar points out)[23], this idolizing of work coincided historically with the start of strenuous efforts to eliminate the human factor in production! Today, we are witnesses to a late stage of this paradoxical process, computerized automation.

What is the future, then, for the work ethic? I believe that we should denounce the idea that work or job equals worth and renounce the idol of work as the meaning of life. But the biblical base, on which the original 'Protestant ethic' was built, is certainly not redundant. Perhaps play and what we now call 'leisure' were somewhat neglected. But as I want to show now, a biblical perspective on work — this 'old ethic' — is highly relevant to today's world.

● **What can be said about paid employment?** (This is *not* the same as 'work'.) The Christian view demands justice in jobs. Without equating jobs with work as such, it is still clear that in today's society, jobs are tremendously important. Many worthwhile schemes are proposed for changing attitudes to work, job-sharing, shorter working weeks and the like.[24] But if we believe that meaningful activity — work — is a vital way of expressing our humanness, then avoiding the spectre of people's energies and talents rotting in the dole (unemployment benefit) line is a priority. For, as currently organized, most of our society's opportunities for some sort of meaningful activity come in the form of jobs.

And not only in the Northern hemisphere. Let us not forget that 'restructuring' of employment in the North has ramifications in the South. Until recently, one could say that much Northern 'de-industrialization' was better seen as a new international division of labour in which manufacturing shifted to the Third World, where labour was cheap. But things are changing. Fewer labels in our clothes say 'Made in Korea (or Hong Kong)'. Why is this? Today, micro-electronic precision stitching and automation is depriving those countries of their comparative advantage.[25]

I leave 'justice in jobs' here, not because it is unimportant, but because little may be said about it which relates directly to IT. Until attitudes and social institutions change — a very long-term process — we should seek justice in the allocation of jobs. Special priority should be given to those worst hit: young people, women, ethnic minorities, those in regions of industrial decline . . . and the South.

● **How does a Christian perspective on work affect attitudes to new technology?** Jesus himself was a skilled worker — a carpenter. In ancient Israel great stress was placed on spirit-filled skill, for instance in the construction of the sacred tent of worship. If work is intended to be a 'labour of love', should we allow deskilling, machine-pacing, and the draining of initiative and responsibility in jobs?

'Of course not,' responds the industrialist indignantly. 'But we have to read the writing on the wall. It says, automate or liquidate.' (He sounds to me like British footballer Kevin Keegan explaining 'progress' to a TV commentator recently: 'It's never nice. But it's gotta come.') Other tempting slogans include: 'People are trouble, machines obey.' Add to this the demand that tasks be broken down into their smallest component parts for greater efficiency, which has been with us for many years, but is boosted by computerization. One begins to see the obstacles to any micro-electronic labour of love.

But the silicon chip does not mean that workers' skills have to be subordinated to a machine, or that their initiative should disappear into the office. At one (USA) Westinghouse plant, 'the office' was one day at its wits' end. The production engineers couldn't persuade their robot to spray-paint an electric motor. They even gave it a second paint gun, to no avail. A young employee, a painter, offered to program the robot for them, and, using his skills, eventually taught the thing to do the job properly.[26]

Take the case of 'expert systems', which give some professional people cause to fear that they will lose even their jobs to the chip. A program called PUFF is being developed to diagnose lung disease. Forty-four rules for diagnosis were obtained from doctors, which gave the computer the chance to 'replace' the expert. But Howard Rosenbrock (from the University of Manchester) shows that the computer may be used to *enhance* the skills of the doctor. His or her work may be speeded by the machine, but there is always room for disagreement. Side-effects of new drugs, or special regional conditions give doctors the chance to retain their expertise.[27]

These kinds of examples may be multiplied. David Noble, in the USA, and Mike Cooley, in the UK, have shown that computer-numerical machine tools may be introduced in ways which enhance and co-operate with the skills of the worker.[28] Similar alternatives have been explored in the automation of clerical work, using word processors. Their operators may end up with *more* varied and responsible jobs. But flexible work organization is required, and a willingness to consider priorities other than profit and productivity. The latter two do not have to be lost just because human priorities, and wider participation in decision-making, are put alongside them.[29]

Finding new ways forward

It is not the quest for greater productivity, using the silicon chip, which is found wanting. It is the denial of human priorities in the development of automated systems which should arouse our indignation. Equally, it is not biblical perspectives on work which are inadequate. No, it is the socially divisive and personally demeaning travesty passing as the 'work ethic' which is an obstacle to justice in jobs and love in labour.

We have to come to terms with the fact of long-term structural unemployment. It is a social scourge not because jobs within the formal economy are intrinsically worthwhile, but because until things change, they are the major means of using human ability and of individuals supporting themselves and their families. So no stone should be unturned in our search for solutions.

With respect to IT, must we lose jobs? The answer is that in many cases jobs will have to be lost. But it is never inevitable. The Peugeot car factory in Ryton, Coventry, recently went over to semi-automated production. Why 'semi-automated'? Because, according to their spokesman, jobs could be retained this way. They say they are rediscovering the importance of 'human' resources.[30] Different strategies may be pursued, not simply to shore up 'dead' industries, but to use human ability in creative harness with new technology.

Moreover, the possibilities for an IT-based job generation should be investigated. New kinds of services may well be the basis of employment expansion. This goes beyond the much-touted tourism and fast-food route. The 'self-servicing' in education, medicine, shopping and other domestic areas could stimulate growth in *manufacturing*.

The other question of course is, can we save skills? David Bleakley, for many years a trades unionist in Ulster, agrees that micro-technology is transforming our world beyond recognition. But as a Christian he says that new technology should be carefully controlled and 'kept compatible with the human needs of the society in which it takes root'.[31]

But how do we do this? Surely we should support all efforts to 'humanize' work. One of the most obvious means is through new technology agreements. Remember the Courage brewery? It was the wide participation of workers which eased the transition to high-technology production, and agreement that workers should retain responsibilities and initiative within a flexible organization. Labour unions such as (the British) APEX produce guidelines on job design. The idea is that management and workers co-operate in ensuring that jobs are satisfying, make full use of ability, and allow access to facilities for enhancing skills and career prospects.[32] Recall the Swedish case as well. There are signs of hope! Let us work with them!

We do not know the future. But trends such as robotics and telecommuting show that we are face to face with immense changes. They offer great challenges for society, politics, and ethics, not just economics. What happens will be the result of many, many decisions. Your decisions and mine.

Being answerable for change within God's world should spur us to an urgent quest for justice in jobs and love in labour. If we do not shape technology by our 'old ethic', it will be shaped by the false demands of the silicon idol. And that is a less-than-human option.

Notes

1 Work Research Unit, *Meeting the Challenge of Change: Case Studies*, HMSO, 1982

2 *The Guardian*, 8 October 1985

3 Colin Gill, *Work, Unemployment and the New Technology*, Polity Press, 1985, page 72

4 Shirley Williams, *A Job to Live*, Penguin, 1985, page 57

5 This is discussed in Gill (see above), page 86

6 Michael Rader, 'Social effects of CAD: current trends and forecasts for the future', in Liam Bannon (and other eds) *Information Technology: Impact on the Way of Life*, Tycooly, 1982

7 No doubt this figure is higher now. This fact was gleaned from *The Observer* (Technology Extra), 11 September 1983

8 Quoted from 'Camilla' in a video, 'Using office automation', TV Choice (London)

9 Capital per head is for offices one tenth what it is in industry. See Gunter Friedrichs and Adam Schaff (eds), *Microelectronics and Society: For Better or Worse*, Pergamon, 1982, page 11

10 Suzanne Iacono and Rob Kling, 'Changing office technology and the

transformation of office work', forthcoming in Laurence Erlbaum (ed.) *Technology and the Transformation of Office Work*, New Jersey, 1985

11 Stephen Bevan, *Secretaries and Typists: the Impact of Office Automation*, University of Sussex: Institute of Manpower Studies, 1985

12 *The Guardian*, 8 October 1985

13 Quoted by Jane Barker and Hazel Downing in Donald MacKenzie and Judy Wajcman, *The Social Shaping of Technology*, Open University Press, 1985, page 160

14 Quoted by Hazel Downing in Tom Forester (ed.), *The Microelectronics Revolution*, Blackwell, page 284

15 *The Times*, 1 May 1984

16 Elia Zureik (see chapter 1, note 5), page 6

17 'Long waves' are part of a theory which originated with Russian economist Nikolai Kondratiev. Christopher Freeman accepts part of his argument and explains it in Pauline Marstrand (ed.), *New Technology and the Future of Work and Skills*, Pinter, 1984

18 Clive Jenkins and Barrie Sherman, *The Collapse of Work*, Eyre-Methuen, 1979

19 Jonathan Gershuny and Ian Miles, *The New Service Economy*, Pinter, 1983

20 See Colin Gill (above)

21 Tony Walter, *Hope on the Dole*, SPCK, 1985

22 Quoted in Paul Marshall (and others), *Labour of Love*, Wedge, 1980, page 9

23 Krishan Kumar, 'The social culture of work: work, employment, and unemployment as ways of life', in *New Universities Quarterly*, 34, 1980

24 Michael Moynagh, *Making Unemployment Work*, Lion (in association with the Shaftesbury Project), 1985

25 Juan Rada, 'A Third World Perspective', in Friedrichs and Schaff (note 9)

26 This example is from Tom Forester, *The Information Technology Revolution*, Blackwell, 1985, page 478

27 H. H. Rosenbrock, 1984, 'Designing automated systems: must skills be lost?', in Pauline Marstrand (note 17), page 130

28 David Noble, 'Social choice in machine design', reprinted in MacKenzie and Wajcman (note 13), and Mike Cooley, *Architect or Bee?*, Langley Technical Services, 1980

29 This is explained further in Council for Science and Society, *New Technology, Work, and Skill*, CSS, 1981

30 *Yorkshire Post*, 1 November 1985

31 David Bleakley, *In Place of Work: the Sufficient Society*, SCM, 1981, page 6

32 *Job Design and New Technology*, APEX, 1985

3
Cable, communication and control

Music, sky-diving, and a 'cable carnival' greeted the birth of Coventry Cable, England, in September 1985. The company is out to prove that the British public really wants sixteen TV channels, and to disprove prior pessimism about cable's future. When I visited Coventry Cable recently, I was impressed with their energy, vision, professionalism and commitment. They are in no doubt that this new technology points the way to tomorrow's world.

A much bigger event — the National Cable Television Convention in Dallas, May 1980 — was hailed as the birth of the new age of television. Suddenly, an old idea had a new lease of life. TV signals would be sent down cables, rather than transmitted to rooftop aerials. Since then, companies have crowded to 'get in on the act', been trampled in the rush, or have stumbled into action.

Cable television has been described as the 'Trojan horse' of the new age.[1] It enters our homes under the guise of 'more entertainment, more choice for viewers'. But cable television is *not* television, at least as we know it today. It is much more than twenty-four-hour rock music, sport, or films. It could become a new major channel of communication, like roads, railways, or telephone lines before it.

Cable television promises (or threatens!) not just old-fashioned general, one-way *broadcasting*, but specific, two-way *narrowcasting*. Our chance has come to answer back to the tube! In Columbus, Ohio, cable subscribers have even had the opportunity to vote on how the soap opera should develop! In Reading, Pennsylvania, house-bound elderly people were linked with each other and with a community centre to make their own live programme.

Cable television is only one — but perhaps the most significant — long-term development in new telecommunications. Much of the latent potential of information technology depends on the establishment of cable. A tremendous amount of digital information may be carried this way. Other new communications technologies include direct broadcasting by satellite, and the linking of computers using telephone lines.

Such innovations raise a host of new questions. How does one protect smaller countries and communities from the cultural clout of big-time satellite broadcasting from the USA? What will happen to journalists and the newspaper industry if 'electronic newspapers' — whose text appears on the screen — push out the popular paper which flops through the mailbox? Will the big, traditional TV companies disintegrate under the onslaught of competition from multiple channels — from cable or satellite?

Maybe we already suspect that we suffer from 'information overload'. The 'information explosion' caused by contact between computers and new communications is indeed mind-blowing. But parallel with this is a curious opposite: information *underload*. The sort of information I have in mind is instruction on *how* new communications technologies should be developed. The dazzle of bright new media is matched by the black hole where ethical guidance should be.

Part of the problem is that our traditional ethics — how we decide what is right behaviour — is *personal*. So we ask questions of television such as, 'will my child's development be stunted (by encouraging short attention-spans) or are worthwhile family virtues reflected?'

But wider questions are also appropriate. 'Who owns television?', 'What is the effect of presenting the major means of communication as entertainment?' Add to this further questions relating to *new* communications technologies, 'What will happen to public service broadcasting?', 'Is their distribution just and fair?', and we realize we are looking for long-term, global ethics, not just personal ones.

Of course, there is no shortage of 'information age'

prophets and pundits. Once again, technofreaks and technophobes abound! The University of California's Herbert
Schiller fears for the future which, he warns, will place
immense power in the hands of information-peddling trans-
national corporations. Information now has a price; it is a
commodity. IT will just magnify already existing inequalities
and injustices in access to information. The mega corporations will gobble up smaller ones, consolidating control.
'Dallas' and 'Dynasty' will swamp the screens of the
world.

Massachusetts Institute of Technology's Ithiel de Sola Pool
is disturbed by no such nightmares. According to him, the
downward spiral of prices for IT items means more and more
people will be able to afford a computer communication
hook-up. Cultural diversity within and between nations will
also be possible as costs fall. Individual freedom will be
enhanced. Concentrations of economic or cultural power will
be increasingly vulnerable to challenge as people make their
own choices and obtain more access to information.

In order to get a handle on these huge issues, we must ask
the right kinds of questions. Not 'will cable make a profit?',
but 'who accepts responsibility for its just development?' Not
'can we capture a global market by satellite advertising?', but
'should we expose Togo or Barbados to more consumerism
and fast living?' Not 'how can we best put over this message?',
but 'can we give a voice to the widow, the orphan, or the
stranger within our gate?'

Like it or not, the 'new age' slogan is close to the truth, at
least as far as the potential of new communications technology
is concerned. As in the case of jobs and work, IT seems to
touch every area at once, transforming our taken-for-granted
world. The spectre lurking in that 'new age' phrase is silicon
idolatry. Subverting such digital deities is central to my
strategy. But as we examine cable, along with other new
technologies, we find signs of hope as well as the familiar hall-
marks of hubris. Christians who have always been in the 'communications business' ('in the beginning was the Word')
should be among the first to realize the crucial significance of

these new technologies. Opportunities exist for us to shape the new technologies in a responsible manner. Do we recognize those opportunities? Are we ready for them?

A communications revolution?

Are we on the brink of a communications revolution? Christian Schwartz-Schilling, the government minister in charge of Germany's cable-laying operation, believes so: '. . . current developments in the field of communications have historical meaning equivalent to the appearance of the printed book.'[2]

So do we now say goodbye to Gutenberg, and prepare ourselves for a new era? We shall see. (Don't burn your books yet. You can't curl up with a VDU, still less slip it into the bathroom!) But what was the effect of making printed books cheaply available? It gave people unprecedented access to a mass of material — not least the Bible — which had previously been locked in libraries or chained in the chancel.

Production problems were overcome by print. Distribution was another matter. It still took time for books, papers and pamphlets to get around. But did that matter? There was time to digest the news and the novel, and to discuss it. Early newspapers in fact carried on the tradition of market-place debates. They simply extended the talk on paper. You could find out how others saw things, or go behind the priests to consult the prophets. And you could answer back.

Something rather different happened with the birth of electronic media. More and more, information is created and broadcast by the powerful. And the old distribution problem is overcome. The message is instantly everywhere. Seven days elapsed before the news of George Washington's death in Alexandria was published in New York. But within half an hour of John Kennedy's assassination nearly 75 per cent of American people heard the news. So messages arrive faster. But there's less chance to hear alternative viewpoints. And, how do we answer back?

Some say, of course, that cable TV will now give us that chance to answer back. Here's hoping. But what else can cable do? Three things make it quite different from old-fashioned TV:

● Using cables to carry signals means more channels are available. So the choice can be more varied, and the programmes 'narrowcast' (rather than broadcast) to specific audiences.

● Cable can be two-way, so that it may be used for polling, emergency calls, or requests for information.

● Cable is easily coupled with other kinds of communication. As well as conventional TV material such as films, cable carries radio, newspapers, and digital computer data.

Aside from the entertainment potential, think what cable offers educationally. Already, TV broadcasts give people access to the best teachers, let them actually *see* the real world of cities, mountains, or blood vessels about which they are learning, and even in some cases give ordinary people the chance to help make programmes.

Cable promises — in theory — to take all this far further. Special channels may be designated for educational and social use. No more need to get up at 6.00 a.m. to catch the Open University class! The two-way feature could mean learning *along with* the teacher, rather than passively being broadcast to. And the local aspect means that programmes could cater for the educational needs of specific neighbourhoods or cities. Aerobics in Urdu or Welsh?[3]

Do these sound like 'piped dreams' rather than potential realities? Without doubt, big obstacles stand in the path. To understand the situation, let us consider the way cable has arrived.

Cable has not come to us primarily as a gift to teachers. Originally it was used for improving TV reception in remote mountain regions in the USA. This old idea has been revived for a simple reason: information technology. The Japanese frankly stated their aim in cabling Tama New Town, in northern Tokyo: such a 'wired city' is a 'building block for the information society'.[4] Just as people and towns were once linked by road-building, the new highways are to carry information, fast, and in large quantities.

Although the UK lacks some of the Japanese co-ordination (cable responsibilities fall somewhere between the Home Office and the Department of Trade and Industry), the motive for cable is the same. All the adverts proclaim one message: greater choice for viewers. So TV consumers pay for the cables to be laid. But the other strand in cable is this. Britain, too, wants to be a high-tech society, which calls for the construction of new information highways. When free enterprise is the order of the day, however, we should not look to the state to construct them. Hence the 'Trojan Horse', which is particularly well camouflaged in Britain!

Cable enthusiasts everywhere see the potential for new 'electronic highways', carrying diverse kinds of 'traffic' such as information and services. (This includes the Dutch, the Canadians, and others who have had cable TV for a long time). But if cable represents the highways of the future, then we should ask three questions:

● **Who may use them?** Right now, in most places, cable companies not only own or control the actual cables, satellite dishes and other hardware, but they also control the programming. They decide, within legal limits, who uses the cable infrastructure and what passes down its wires. Access could be denied to a competitor who, say, wished to use the cable for an alternative information service.

In 1982, Richard Robinson, a Californian Democrat, introduced a bill to regulate California's cable industry. He argued that cable should be seen as a public utility (like the telephones), that operation should be separate from control of programming, and that equal access should be granted to California's 'knowledge industries' in order to stimulate cable's wider use.[5] Opposition in the industry was quickly mobilized, and Robinson's bill defeated. No doubt the question will be raised again.

● **Who may not use the new cable highways?** At present, experiments with the most advanced technology have been in fairly well-off suburbs and in new towns such as Higashi Ikoma in Japan or Milton Keynes in England. On a very optimistic estimate, Britain is unlikely to have more than 50 per cent of homes wired up in the foreseeable future. Canada, 'the most wired nation on earth', had 75 per cent of homes with access to cable in 1980.[6]

Those who cannot use cable will therefore be those in rural areas, and the less well-off. The more that useful educational and information services are offered via cable, the greater will be the divide between the 'information-rich' and the 'information-poor'. Is this fair?

● **What can the electronic highway carry?** The answer to this is technical, but has deep social implications. We are already talking about multiple channel, broad bandwidth cable networks. But there are two ways of setting this up. The better known is the 'tree and branch' (TAB) system, where the signals are carried from a 'headend' down a main 'trunk', and distributed down the 'branches' to users — homes and businesses. This technology is proven, and cheaper to install than the other 'switched star' (SS) system. But it has a very limited 'return path', making it difficult to send messages *back*. It is hard to increase its capacity once installed, though this is not so true of the newest systems which are built ready for upgrading.

The switched star, on the other hand, enables point-to-point communications, and is thus more suitable for two-way, interactive use. It is more like the telephone, except that it is far more versatile, and can carry many different kinds of traffic — video library facilities for instance. Unfortunately it is more expensive to install, and adequate switches are hardly out of the test laboratory!

While on the topic of what the highway can carry, we ask, what kind of cables? Again, although co-axial cables have been used until now, we are right on the brink of breakthrough to using fibre optic cables. These are suitable for SS systems, and were first developed in Britain. They allow greater capacity, and less chance of interference. And when we think of the kinds of personal information which could pass through the cables (credit cards, and shopping accounts, for example) it may be more reassuring to know the system is harder to tap!

Who says technology is neutral? Different sorts of social relationships are clearly built into different cable technologies! Much TAB cabling simply perpetuates what we have experienced with broadcasting: 'them' sending messages to 'us'. Switched star, on the other hand, means far more opportunity to answer, for dialogue, to use the network for many other purposes than mere entertainment.

The term 'communications revolution' may or may not be appealing. But the advent of new cable TV networks alone will clearly make huge changes in how we regard 'the box'. Already we have amassed several unanswered questions which apply wherever cable is expanding: what is the new technology *for*, who decides, and who can use it?

There are also other questions which I have not addressed. For instance, 'will cable television mean the end of public service broadcasting, especially as it is known in Europe?' Christopher Martin, director of religious television at the British Independent Broadcasting Authority, has called it the new dissolution of the monasteries. We lose the guardians of the good. Trivia takes over.

Alongside these are unanswerable questions (which are particularly acute for those just beginning the 'new wave' of cabling): will enough people *want* to subscribe and will the wider potential of cable be realized? But there are also other new communications technologies, each laden with queries of their own.

The 'information explosion'

Why do we hear so much about the 'information explosion'? Think of this. We often get news from the Reuters newsdesks around the world. But what has made Reuters into a massive success story in the later twentieth century? Not its news so much as its handling of financial information.

Reuters began by using cable for news in 1851, when a Franco-British cross-channel cable was laid. A hundred years later, its prospects were bleak. Hopes rose through another cable connection, this time supplying news for Manhattan Cable Company in New York. But once into financial information, Reuters did not look back. Their 'electronic market' has turned a struggling news service into a major money-spinner.

Or consider this. Even before American novelist Edward Bellamy wrote his utopia *Looking Backward*, which features a 'cashless society', people dreamed of a world where money transactions are obsolete. But by linking bank computers to store computers — as has happened in some places in the USA for the past decade, and is just starting to happen in Europe — the dream comes true. (The jargon word for this is in fact a nightmare: EFTPOS, 'electronic funds transfer at point of sale'! It may sound convenient, but think of this. You drive up to your smart computerized filling station, pop the nozzle into your tank, and wait. Soon a message flashes up: 'Your account is in the red. We have siphoned the remaining fuel from your tank!')

These are just two examples of the information explosion. Using telephone lines, datalines, satellites, or cable, information travels rapidly from place to place. Electronic mail, encountered in new, high-tech offices, is another example. When an information service like this is offered, for a price, it is often called a VAN or 'value-added network'.

Such vastly increased pace and efficiency of information flow has tremendous advantages. But it also means that it may become less easy to keep track of where the information goes. On an individual level, I have already mentioned how more and more personal details are computerized, which rings warning bells about privacy.

On an international level, the speed and volume of financial transfers via Reuters or SWIFT (another inter-continental data system) means that capital is constantly on the move, and that control of companies shifts to where data is processed. Canadians, for example, are badly worried by the southern flow of data into the USA. They say that they not only lose decision-making power to the city offices of their nearest neighbour, but that they have lost thousands of jobs in data processing.

We can multiply illustrations of the 'information explosion'.

Another route to better understanding is to examine two specific communications technologies.

In 1979 the British Post Office started the world's first two-way, interactive, text-on-television service, 'Prestel'. It connects computer and television via the telephone (using a 'modem' to translate the signals into the right form). Using this system, one can request information of many sorts — weather, stock exchange, plane flights and bookings, and consumer advice. Originally seen as a route to the electronic newspaper, one may also find more bizarre services from Prestel (such as limericks), and, if they get their way, more socially dubious ones such as gambling.

Similar videotex services, such as the German Bildschirmtext, are appearing all over the world. (Japan had a bigger problem than most — how to put 4,000 ideographs on the screen rather than the three dozen letters and numbers that we use!) Businesses use them, and with the recent boom in home computers, many households are also using services such as Prestel.

People can find their way into Prestel and other videotex networks illegally. Several 'hackers' have been prosecuted in Britain for entering private databases. But privacy is not the only problem.

Control is another concern. As with cable, should the operator be allowed to determine how the system is used? And even if anyone is allowed to use it (Prestel was obliged to 'open up' after an aborted attempt to act as 'gatekeeper') other questions about content arise. They are not unique to videotex. Whatever the new medium, we must ask, for instance, 'can it be a soapbox?', 'will pornography be permitted?'

Such questions certainly surface in the case of direct broadcasting by satellite. DBS is growing fast. Some see it as a threat to 'wired society' dreams if people choose to pick up satellite signals themselves, rather than via the cable station. More than a million satellite dishes already grace the rooftops of American buildings. British rules restricting satellite reception were relaxed during 1985,[7] allowing hotels, apartment blocks and others who can afford the dish to receive channels such as Music Box, The Movie Channel, and Sky.

Technofreaks greet satellite TV as a bright dawn. 1960s media prophet Marshall McLuhan called its result the 'global village'. But others have justified forebodings about DBS — especially its capacity to enter distant homes with alien messages. *They* see telecommunications as the 'bully of the global village'. Many Europeans are worried by what they regard as a threat from American satellite companies. Coronet, for instance, has been dubbed the 'coca-cola satellite'. This particular American 'bird' would be very glad to fly over Europe.[8]

The pejorative term used for such potential media power is 'cultural imperialism'. How might Western nations take to Libya, Iran, or the Soviet Union invading their domestic screens with propaganda? Or vice versa. Would the Ayatollah not be distressed to see 'Miss World' arriving via rooftop dishes?

Those least able to resist such an imposition of foreign values and lifestyles are nations in the Southern hemisphere. Whether in the Caribbean or the African sub-continent, Third World nations are at a distinct disadvantage when it comes to new telecommunications. Their finances limit them just to receive, not transmit, satellite signals. They risk losing their cultural identity and independence to the big powerful Western communications companies.

But the Third World suffers from the impact of the 'information explosion' in two other ways. The American 'Landsat' satellites (which survey rather than broadcast) can analyze mineral and agricultural resources in a detailed way — even field by field. Anyone can ask for this information, free of charge. But, not anyone can *interpret* the satellite's bleeps into useful maps. Northern commodity dealers have that capacity. The Southern nations themselves often do not. Given today's pernicious trend towards using food as a political lever, this is a troublesome development.

The other danger for the Third World is similar to that facing Canada: data flows across national borders. Data on markets, technology, and credit assessments is very valuable to businesses. Fears grow about the American near-monopoly of databases and equipment. Again, this simply aggravates the North-South dependency divide.[9]

The information explosion shatters many time-honoured traditions, respects few national boundaries, and raises urgent questions about licensing and limits. Is it not enough that the growth of IT outstrips the pace of political regulation? How much more tricky to deal with its telecommunications aspects, which simply step outside conventional politics altogether?

How can we cope? There is only one way. The shrug of despair or the rush to regulate will not do. We have to go behind economics, behind politics. We must explore *ethical* questions. What is it for? Who decides? Is it fair? What is the right way forward?

Responsible technology?

Information technology seems to hit us from all sides at once. Its effects are long-term, and global, immediate, and personal. No one has yet come up with a satisfactory definition of 'information', but we have massive databases to store it and megacomputers to process it. We are amazed at the wizardry which bounces Coventry Cable's TV channels off a satellite in geo-stationary orbit 23,000 miles above the earth. And minds boggle at the power vested in the huge telecommunications transnationals, within which so many crucial decisions seem to be taken.

In such a context, how can we talk of 'responsible technology'? What problems confront us as we try to discover how new technology is shaped? And how may we share in that shaping?

● **Do we actually understand the technologies?** There is a tendency to be 'bold but blinkered'. The Western world is moving jerkily but determinedly into the 'information era', sure that the future lies there. Japan leads the way as far as planning goes. The Ministry of International Trade and Industry (MITI) believes that overall co-ordination will work. But in many other countries, especially where 'deregulation' and 'free enterprise' is the order of the day, new technology is allowed to find its own place.

Much legislation is simply unclear as to what satellite broadcasting or cable means. In Britain, cable regulation is thoroughly ambiguous. Is it television, or not? Of course, the medium *is* novel. It combines the potential pluralism of many new channels with the logical monopoly of the cable company. You cannot give more than one franchise for a given area. So should it be regulated like public service broadcasting, like publishing, or as a 'common carrier' (like the telephone)? In Britain and other countries, cable company directors are in an extremely powerful position. The burden of deciding who uses this 'electronic highway' falls largely on them.

Is this 'bold but blinkered' approach inevitable? When motor cars first made their appearance on British roads, the worst hazard was the dust thrown up by cars using unmade roads. Would their development have been blocked or re-channelled if someone had foreseen smog, lead poisoning, urban congestion, or even that atrophied condition, 'commuter's leg'?

This is the dilemma of control. When a technology is new, we cannot foresee its social and environmental effects. But by the time they become apparent, it is too late or too difficult to do anything about it. The idea of responsible technology calls for something more than 'let's see what happens', though even that represents a *choice*. Wherever possible, the chance to redirect the technology as it is developed should be built in.[10]

For instance, the British government requirement that cable systems be upgradable (from TAB to SS) is a small step in the right direction. Beyond this, constant review, which bears in mind social as well as economic priorities, ought to be a basic aspect of regulation. Britons can rejoice that Ugly George's porn channel has been refused entry. But at present, few countries have any public authority with any real power to regulate new technology more widely. We may have cause to regret this later.

Another point, of course, is that we are always in a tearing rush to be first, to get an edge over others. Is this the route to responsible technology? The German Social Democrats and the Green Party are saying 'slow down'. Give us time to check what other alternatives are available before we commit ourselves to this massive cabling project. Nora and Minc, authors of the French report on '*L'informatisation*' argue that 'in order to make the information society possible it is necessary to have knowledge but also to have time'.[11] It does not follow that *we* can know and learn overnight just because computers can work fast. Change should be paced.

● **How do we treat information?** We face the problem of 'commodities or resources'. Again, the fact that it is hard to define 'information' makes the question more difficult. From an economist's point of view, information itself cannot be a scarce resource. If I tell you that Britain has more home micros per head than any other nation, you have 'gained' that information but I have 'lost' nothing. Who 'owns' my date of marriage? The registrar? My wife and I? These are technical points. The issue is this. By restricting *access* to information, people turn it into a scarce resource, something to be bought and sold *like* a commodity.

We see this happen when a rich nation gains information which would be valuable to a poorer country, for instance agricultural information. Access to information is also restricted when free public libraries are replaced by electronic databases, and handsome fees charged. If new educational and information services are offered via cable TV, only those who live in the right area, and are able to afford the subscription, will be able to benefit from them. Even the chance to make a living could depend upon access to cable. The development of intermediate services for home security, home shopping, and other services may happen as cable is established. Some may be prevented from starting such businesses due to lack of access, or to inadequate infrastructure.

Not only jobs but democracy too depends on an informed electorate. The USA has long prided itself on government openness. So the transfer of public information — whether on health, industrial performance, or Third World aid — to the market-place, with a price-tag, is abhorrent to many. A 1979 White House conference on library and information services, for instance, resolved that free public access to information be maintained and extended, and that Congress should 'foster broad public participation in federal government by subsidizing the sale of documents and maintaining the system of regional depository libraries'.[12] As yet there is nothing approaching this in the UK.

Economists may wrangle endlessly about whether information has become a 'factor of production' like land, labour or capital. But the fact remains that access to information is more and more important in today's world. It is increasingly treated as a commodity.

In ancient Israel, the stress was reversed. Resources came before commodities. For the people of the Old Testament, this meant that access to *land* was crucial. They affirmed as a basic truth that 'the earth is the Lord's, and all it contains'. But they also knew that their God-given responsibility was to be stewards of the earth for the good of all. Access to resources was biblically prior to ownership. And even ownership was not about the right of disposal, but about responsible administration and distribution.[13]

Old Testament ethics thus seem highly appropriate for us today — assuming that access to information and access to land are comparable! This perspective suggests that all efforts to *open* access to information should be applauded. Should we not seek mechanisms to ensure that nations whose land is subject to remote sensing by satellites should have a right to that information? Should we not press politicians to make new media such as cable TV into 'common carriers', so that, as with telephones, all may use them?

In the Old Testament securing the physical and social life of each *family* was paramount. But if, due to the consequences of their failure to live by God's directives families found themselves in dire straits, special help was available. And beyond this lay the so-called 'jubilee', divinely designed to prevent the accumulation of the bulk of resources in the hands of a minority. In that 'jubilee' year all property was returned to its original owner-steward. Again, the aim was to protect families. Jesus once stood up in his home town and announced that the jubilee had come.[14] By doing so he both underlined its continuing significance, and also pointed to its spiritual and future meaning.

● **Monologue or dialogue: are we *communicating*?** One could say that the printed book and the newspaper extended the practice of talking together. You could still have *honesty* within trusting relationships ('speaking the truth in love' as it is called elsewhere). The electronic media, on the other hand, increasingly transmit messages from powerful commercial interests into private homes. Monologue replaces dialogue. The activity is one-way.

This is obvious on a global level. The identity of small countries is threatened by big-time satellite communications. Privately-owned media (press, radio, publishing, television, records, and video) are becoming more and more concentrated in their ownership. The Western world alone is the market for eighty US communications corporations which control three quarters of the international communications market.[15] 80 per cent of Latin American television programmes (*Route 66*, *Bonanza*, *The Flintstones*) is American.[16] And apart from the rare series such as the British Channel Four's *Utopia Limited*, we seldom hear a Southern hemisphere view of the North. '*Co*mmunication' is all too often a misnomer. It is one-way.

Anyone watching events such as the World Cup or Superbowl is treated not only to screen sport, but to the hoardings and billboards of the 'global persuaders'. Beer and jeans, cars and computers get their plug. Advertising, and, with the advent of satellite, programming, is done more and more with an international audience in mind. Big, powerful companies reach directly into the homes of their anonymous audiences.

We have already suggested that from a Christian perspective such a gross imbalance of power is far from ideal. The voice of the ethnic minority, or of the small and poor Third World country, is drowned in the noise of commercial TV. In the Western world, television especially claims to speak on behalf of the 'national community'. Programme titles such as *Nationwide* suggest that there is an identifiable 'we' out there.[17] But the inclusive 'we' is misleading. Television exists in a fragmented and divided world. On the other hand, for many in the private suburban rabbit-warrens, the television is the only thing they have in common. But when only one sort of view comes across, and not the real diversity of opinion, viewpoint, and conviction, once again the idea of 'communication' remains unrealized.

Cable TV may in the end do little to change this situation — even with its local and interactive potential. For cable still must succeed as a commercial venture. Without specific safeguards, the major satellite channels may squeeze out real choice. In the Qube cable experiment in Columbus, Ohio, it was found that genuine 'community advancement' had a low profile.

Anyone who wishes to get involved in the new media should be aware of, and try to work against, the 'monologue syndrome'. Many religious programmes have unfortunately fallen into this trap. (One of the major public concerns in Europe at the prospect of receiving American satellite programmes is this 'monologue syndrome'. The 'electronic church', with its 'prime time preachers' and 'televangelism' is a blessing many would rather do without!) At the same time, I must mention efforts being made to find alternative uses for new media in the context of 'Christian communication'. In Britain, videotex is being explored as a means of raising questions of faith in a 'discussion' mode.[18]

If we believe that talking together, hearing others' viewpoints, and giving a voice to the voiceless is important, then we enter a real struggle. The tide is running against us. *C*ommunication is still more of a hope than a reality.

Obstacles and opportunities

Technology shows its two faces once again in new telecommunications. There is, apparently, very little we can do to shape these mushrooming media. But although the obstacles are real, the hope that one day genuine *c*ommunication will occur is no less real. Though that day will not dawn through human effort, human effort is required of all who hope in God's promise. There are opportunities as well as obstacles.

Perhaps the biggest temptation to hopeless inertia is inspired by the spectacle of the Southern hemisphere at the mercy of the North. Big corporations hold sway, and seem to be answerable to no one but themselves.

Opportunities do exist to raise people's awareness of the issues, and to alert governments to the effects of their policies. Whatever their shortcomings and demerits, the work of the 'Brandt Commission', or of the 'McBride Commission' — a UNESCO team which discussed the telecommunications problem — should be heeded.[19] Not that such commissions have all the answers. The proposed 'new international communication and information order' may well be unworkable or unwise.

But consciences may yet be stirred by attention being drawn to the plight of many nations, economically dependent on the North and dominated by the advertising-sponsored programmes, who receive their 'aid' in the form of unsafe or inappropriate technology, and are being enticed to enter the one-way street of Western-style industrial development. By outlining an alternative, however utopian it may sound, one may catch a vision of a more just society.

Christians, moreover, are mandated to pray 'Your kingdom come. Your will be done on earth as it is in heaven.' Where is the clause excluding the Third World from that prayer? Is it any surprise that prayer is always a priority in biblical politics?

One of the biggest obstacles to responsible technology in the Northern hemisphere is the pace of change. It is hard to keep up! Add to this the trend towards putting a price on information access, official failure to understand the new technology, and the power of the media barons, and the prospects are daunting.

But the new technologies *do* offer new opportunities, if only we can grasp them! Signs of hope exist! Many new cable operators are looking for ideas to make use of the expanded capacity cable offers. In Britain, companies in Aberdeen,

Coventry, Glasgow and Swindon have shown interest in programmes from black and Asian groups, and from voluntary organizations.

We should do all we can to ensure that 'public access' becomes a (statutory) reality. In Holland, television has operated in a pluralist fashion for some time. Families of all the dominant religious and political groups are represented in, and help to pay for, Dutch television.

Here is a further example. A recent conference on 'community computing' brought together activists committed to the idea of opening up computing power to those often excluded from it.[20] Although somewhat eccentric, a 'community memory' project has already run for several years in San Francisco. It operates as an exchange for everything from Greek cooking classes to advice about nuclear power or natural childbirth.

Tired of a bland presentation of their faith on television, Christians may themselves wish to take advantage of the new technologies. Plans are advancing in Swindon for a 'Family Channel' to co-ordinate programming in association with one of the big cable companies. On an explicit Christian base, the idea is to offer a wide range of family entertainment, children's programmes, educational, social, and news features. A panel discussion of embryo research (organized by some of the same people) has already been shown on Swindon cable.

The danger of grasping new opportunities in telecommunications is that we get sucked into silicon idolatry. It is very subtle. But should we not also stand back and ask what basic human needs are served by having twenty rather than four or five TV channels? And even if some justification can be found, should we not be concerned when we read in the cable literature about 'consumers', 'units', 'households', 'purchasers', but little about 'people', 'families', or 'homes'?[21]

The original technological idol was erected on the Plain of Shinar. It was called the Tower of Babel. Proud self-sufficiency and delusions of deity were its building bricks. Confusion of communication was its divine punishment.

Centuries later, the prophet Zephaniah promised a great

reversal. Voices would one day blend in mutual understanding. Undistorted communication would accompany united worship of God. This happened at Pentecost, itself a foretaste of another future.

Meanwhile, Babel, or Babylon, distinguished itself by continuing to symbolize shameless pretensions, gross injustice, and a low view of human life. Hebrews exiled there hung their harps on the willows. How could they sing in a strange land? But another prophet, Jeremiah, roused them from apathy. They should work together for justice and truth even *in* Babylon. 'Seek the welfare of the city,' he told them, 'and pray for it'. We are still exiles in Babylon.

Notes

1 Stuart Hoover, *The Electronic Giant: a Critique of the Telecommunications Revolution from a Christian Perspective*, Brethren Press, 1982, page 95

2 Quoted in Gary Geipl, 'Medienpolitik', *Channels*, May/June 1985, page 42

3 The educational potential is discussed by Robin McCron 'New technologies: new opportunities?', *Journal of Educational Television*, 1984, 10, 1, pages 7–18

4 Quoted in Ibarra Gonzalez in W. H. Dutton (and other eds) *The Wired City* (forthcoming)

5 See Robert Kahn, 'The impact of cable' in Tom Forester (ed.) *The Information Technology Revolution*, Blackwell, 1985, page 150

6 Brian Murphy, *The World Wired Up*, Comedia, 1983, page 51

7 *Sunday Times* report, 26 May 1985

8 Richard Spandler, 'In Europe, cable and DBS start even', *Channels*, March/April 1985, page 32

9 See Rita Cruise O'Brien, 'New problems in North-South relations', in Paul Sieghart (ed.) *Microchips With Everything*, Comedia, 1983, and Juan Rada, 'The Third World', in Gunter Friedrichs and Adam Schaff (eds) *Microelectronics and Society: For Better or Worse*, Pergamon, 1982

10 This is discussed by David Collingridge, *The Social Control of Technology*, Open University Press, 1980

11 Simon Nora and Alain Minc, *The Computerisation of Society*, MIT Press, 1980

12 Herbert Schiller, *Who Knows: Information in the Age of the Fortune 500*, Norwood Ablex, 1981, page 66

13 See Christopher Wright, *Living as the People of God*, Inter-Varsity Press, 1983

14 Luke 4:19

15 Cees Hamelink, *Cultural Autonomy in Global Communications*, Longman, 1983, quoted in Howard Davis and Richard Scase, *Western Capitalism and State Socialism*, Blackwell, 1985, page 175

16 Jeremy Tunstall, *The Media are American*, Columbia University Press, 1977, pages 39–40

17 Roger Silverstone, 'The right to speak: an apologetic for television documentary', *Media, Culture and Society*, 1984, 5, pages 137–54

18 Michael Parsons has produced *Viewdata and the Churches*, available from North of England Institute for Christian Education, Carter House, Pelau Leazes Lane, Durham DH1 1TB, UK

19 Sean McBride (ed), *Many Voices, One World*, UNESCO, 1980

20 Jenny Mill, 'Solving social problems with a box of tricks', *Computing*, 10, October 1985, pages 14–15

21 See Robin McCron (note 3), page 16

4

To the fourth and fifth generation

Imagine that you are unemployed in Britain in the 1990s. You go to claim your benefit at the social security office. Gone is the tired and harassed clerk; instead, you are confronted by a computer keyboard and screen. You type in your responses to its questions, and from its intricate memory of benefit rules and regulations out pops the correct entitlement statement.

This is no futurist dream. The 'Alvey' programme is paying for research into such 'expert' computers, and the Department of Health and Social Security (DHSS) hopes the national system will be installed by 1990.[1] A massive integrated network of computers will hold all the relevant information. Just one element, the index based on national insurance numbers, will be the largest database in Britain, containing 130 million million characters.

We can view the computerization of welfare benefits in different ways. The computer industry stands to gain because standards will be set. A sort of computer Esperanto will allow many different machines to 'talk' with each other.[2] The DHSS will save money because fewer staff will be needed. From the viewpoint of employees, of course, that means lost jobs. And the whole operation is a huge headache for security. Those running the system fear hackers and fraud, and have already set up an electronic security team. Those whose names and records are in the system will want assurances about who sees their personal details and why.

But the reason we are interested in the DHSS computers is this. It illustrates the fact that many more people are coming into direct contact with new technology. In an experiment at eight centres, involving nearly 400 people, researchers found that most *preferred* their contact with the computer to that

with people! Why? Although most were unemployed and un-
familiar with computers, they learned more about social
security and enjoyed using the machines. It was worth their
while, for half of them discovered they were entitled to more
benefits. And, best of all, they received them right away.[3]

There's no escape! Very quickly, information technology is
becoming an unavoidable aspect of conducting our everyday
business. Everyone tells us we have to prepare to live with new
machines; not just machines which increase our physical
powers — cars, washing machines, pneumatic drills — but
machines which mimic human powers of reason.

Many are disturbed by this thought. Surely, they say, there
must be some difference between digital deftness and the wide
horizons of my creative imagination? Doesn't the artificial
intelligence (AI) movement simply want to narrow the gap
between machines and human beings? Isn't all this a reduc-
tionist threat to traditional Christian views of human dignity?

This is just one of the issues facing us in this chapter, which
focusses on the wider cultural impact of computers. What is
the meaning of the computer for our human self-image, our
significant symbols, and our souls?

Consider this question. What will happen as we learn to
communicate with computers, whether for medical diagnosis,
welfare benefits, or education? Can machines really be 'user-
friendly'? (Some unhappy patrons of automatic bank tellers
doubt it, apparently. When the polite instructions dry up
abruptly with REFER TO BANK, annoyed customers may be
heard cursing the machine which has 'swallowed', 'chewed
up' or 'snatched away' their card. Frustrated telephone-callers
leave sarcastic messages: 'Hello, answering machine. This is a
human being speaking. Tell your master I rang.')[4]

Children in the earliest grades of school are now being
exposed to keyboards and VDUs. But what will result?
Deepened social relationships? Or an impersonal society,
where people no longer know how to talk with each other?
Elevation to a new and exciting plane of joyful problem-
solving activity? Or a shrivelled parody of human experience,
operating only on the level of data and information?

Another question is, are computers becoming the cultural symbol of our age? Will they affect the way we see ourselves, as we exchange a 'clockwork image' for an 'information image'? Will computers pace and regulate our lives, as the clock does in industrial society?

Beyond this, will computers make society even more secular? Will the calculating approach to life, seen so clearly in the growth of capitalism and of science, receive a new boost? Will religious belief and moral codes be further eroded by a new form of secularity — what Os Guinness calls the 'acid rain of the spirit'?[5]

I believe that some of these are false fears, even though they seem real enough to those who have them! In some cases, the technology is misunderstood, or the claims for it are exaggerated. In other cases, people are underestimated, or the history of Christianity is seen too negatively. The answers to yet other questions are simply unavailable: we don't know.

But for those with a high view of 'humanness', who see people as the 'image of God', these questions are all serious, all significant. Should we not be deeply concerned about the way society is going, about the role of technology, and what it means to real people in their everyday lives? If so, we will want to explore these questions. But if so, equally, we shall not be content with mere analysis.

One tremendously influential area is education. Both technofreaks and technophobes agree that much is at stake here. Giving more and more people access to computer power is one thing. Helping them see the wider context of cultural impact and ethical query is another. At this level fine opportunities exist to go beyond analysis to practical proposals.

The fifth frontier

The race to the 'fifth frontier' began in earnest only in May 1981. A Japanese research paper arrived on the desk of Michael Dertouzos, director of the Massachusetts Institute of Technology's computer laboratory. It outlined plans for building supercomputers, thousands of times faster than today's, and computers embodying 'artificial intelligence'.

To Dertouzos, it appeared that the Japanese had stolen his ideas: 'I looked at it and I started panicking, panicking, panicking . . .'[6]

Why was he so bothered? Let him explain: 'This assault is far more serious to our future than the automobiles sold from Japan, because the computer is at the root of every major future change.' One's power in the world depends, increasingly, on being ahead in the 'information revolution'.

The Americans rapidly roused themselves. Huge research co-operatives, and the Pentagon's powerful Defence Advanced Research Projects Agency (DARPA) rolled into action. Not to be outdone, Britain launched her own 'Alvey' computer research programme, taking a leaf out of Japan's advance planning book. France, too, saw the future in *la cinquième génération*, forming a group known as SICO (*Club Systèmes Informatiques de la Connaissance*) to meet the Japanese challenge. Other nations are following suit. The fifth frontier is the goal.

What is so magic about this fifth frontier? According to one definition, AI is 'the science of making machines do things that would require intelligence if done by men'.[7] On the one hand, a breakthrough to AI would be to realize a dream held since the time of the Greeks, if not before. On the other, think of the tremendous *political* power which could be conferred on those possessing AI. Then the fact that many of the world's leading scientists believe AI to be within our grasp, using supercomputers, does indeed appear to be 'magic'.

So-called fifth generation computers will go beyond today's (very powerful) mathematically-based logic. Scientists hope they will be able to understand natural languages (presumably including Scouse, Scots, and Quebec French?), understand their own principles of operation, and have a grasp of knowledge appropriate to their particular area of application.

No one can afford to be without this! An American duo, Feigenbaum and McCorduck, who have produced a highly influential account of *The Fifth Generation*, alert us to the consequences of missing the boat: those who do will be 'stranded in a quaint museum of the intellect, forced to live . . . on the charity of those who understand the real dimensions of the revolution'.[8]

With this kind of threat, the priorities of the UK 'Alvey' project come as no surprise. It is committed to research into Very Large Scale Integration (VLSI) — superchips — software engineering, human/machine interfaces (including voice and language recognition), and expert systems.

The 'human/machine interface' research, crudely put, is making computers more 'user-friendly'. We already have cars which 'talk' to us, telling us when we are low on fuel. (I even heard of a device for warning drivers of their drowsiness!) How much better when we can talk to the machine (I have a thing or two to tell mine!).

What are 'expert systems'? They have, in fact, already been encountered in the computerization of the British welfare system. According to Donald Michie, of the Turing Institute in Strathclyde, Scotland, an expert system 'embodies organized knowledge concerning some specific area of human expertise *sufficient to be able to do duty as a skilful and cost-effective consultant*'.[9] As he points out, in everyday life, people don't often want to know the square root of 35,769. Rather, we want to know, 'what's wrong with this patient?', 'would this be a good spot to drill a well?', 'who killed the sheriff?'[10] Until recently, we have mainly used computers for routine work. Now, we may consult them as 'experts'.

Have you ever tried to discover why your goldfish is listless or lacking appetite? I have a brother-in-law whose research may one day solve your problem (though not, by then, your goldfish's). He is working on an 'expert system' to help diagnose fish disease. The idea is this. He builds up a collection of all the 'rules of thumb' which experts use to determine what is wrong when fish are unwell. He gradually forms them into a logically-connected pattern, from which the computer makes inferences. *If* the fish has had contact with such-and-such a parasite . . . *If* the water temperature was unusually low . . . and so on, *then*, it's likely that the fish is suffering from this condition.

My relative is among those coming to be called 'knowledge

engineers'. Perhaps when the fifth generation arrives, his machine will detect whether it is dealing with someone who knows a lot about fish disease (who may ask the computer how it reached its conclusions), or a humble fish farmer (who will be more interested in what's wrong and what can be done).

Other developments include teaching computers to recognize objects and processes using a TV 'eye'. This may be used, for instance, by detectives trying to identify faces from fuzzy photos (such as newspaper images). All this sounds scarcely credible (at least to those still coming to terms with cars or TV!). But enough sane people are working on AI projects to suggest that the promise is not empty. If realized, it will be very handy.

We become wary, however, when we read on the jacket of the Michie and Johnston book that 'poverty, hunger, disease and political strife are widespread, and new technology is often held responsible, but now solutions to these problems are within sight, and the solutions are going to come from computers'.

A leading critic of such extravagant effusions (himself an AI pioneer) is Joseph Weizenbaum. He scathingly dismisses the 'artificial intelligentsia' which generates the hype about the 'fifth generation'. He worries about two things in particular: human dignity and human life.

Does AI pose a threat to human dignity? Could human minds be replaced by machines? Weizenbaum's fears were initially aroused by the public reaction to a program he wrote, called ELIZA.[10] Intended to show how people could 'converse' with a computer, it parodied Rogerian counselling methods. 'I have always had family problems.' 'Tell me about your family.' And so on. (At that time, of course, computers did not have the wit to avoid errors like 'How do you know you didn't sleep last night?')

What alarmed Weizenbaum was the overblown promises others attached to his program (that it really 'understood' natural language), the enthusiasm of psychiatrists to automate their practice by using it, and the way its users became emotionally involved with it. Why was this a threat to human dignity? Because people allowed themselves to ascribe far greater powers of reason to the computer than was warranted, and simultaneously allowed their own capacities to be downgraded.

But note where the 'threat' originated: with the people, not in the machines themselves. I shall come to the 'people' problem. Let us first dispense with the 'machine' problem.

This field is fraught with potential pitfalls. We just do not know where AI research will eventually lead. But as Keele University's brain scientist, Donald MacKay, says, 'At most, the science fiction achievement of "artificial consciousness" could only upgrade our respect for the potentialities of "machinery", and why should anyone object in principle to that?'[12] Let us avoid the perils of premature panic, since no Christian teaching demands we rule out in advance the possibility that humans could create thinking machines.

On the other hand, as a Christian I do want to stress the special qualities of human beings, including our responsibility to God to use our minds aright. This has two major implications. First, we must eschew views which diminish that dignity we have conferred on us as God's creatures. A philosopher's rhetorical question says it all: 'does *God* see human beings as information processors made of meat?'[13] Second, we must avoid ascribing to the machines capacities or qualities they do not possess. A user-friendly machine cannot love you.

I wish that a greater number of people were more concerned by the other major threat posed by AI research, the threat to human life. Military funding is crucial to AI research, just as in general the booms and slumps in the electronics industry can be traced to the waves of defence spending.

Feigenbaum and McCorduck make this clear: 'The so-called smart weapons of 1982, for all their sophisticated modern electronics, are really just extremely complex wind-up toys compared to the weapons systems that will be possible in a decade if intelligent information processing systems are applied to the defence problems of the 1990s.' They laud the Israeli achievement of shooting down seventy-nine Syrian planes with no losses to themselves, using electronic battle management.

Newsweek magazine also frankly uncovered this vital aspect of AI research in a 1983 cover story: 'Once they are in place, these technologies will make possible an astonishing new breed of weapons and military hardware. Smart robot weapons — drone aircraft, unmanned submarines, and land vehicles — that combine artificial intelligence and high-powered computing and can be sent off to do jobs that now involve human risk. This is a very sexy area to the military . . .'[14]

It must be noted that the European 'Eureka' high-tech research programme, though ostensibly civil, is also likely to be driven by similar military imperatives.[15]

In a moment we shall examine the kinds of 'decisions' which computers may be expected to take in the military context. But by contrast let us remember that AI is not *only* a military tool (or toy). It may be a threat to life; it can also enhance life. The Edinburgh-based 'computing and social responsibility' group argue that AI should be used for the disabled, for example in making text-to-speech systems for the blind, or to broaden the world of the mentally handicapped.[16] Research in this area is a real sign of hope.

Machines and persons: friends or foes?

IT gives a new urgency to the old question: what is the proper relationship between machines and persons? Are we friends or foes? Technology is often seen as a tyrant. Is this a false fear? Without referring to the more frightening Franken-stein version, we can see how our own creations have turned against us.

We are increasingly isolated in the modern world. Our daily clock-and-car-bound routines cut us off from the seasons and the smells of nature.[16] New technology seems in some cases to take this further. People are split away from their skills as machine tools are computerized. Others find they have more communication, but less *contact* with people as cable TV and electronic mail spread. So much for our created unity with the earth, and the Christian emphasis on the quality of human relationships.

Could AI take this unhappy process a stage further? What makes us special as human beings is that we are what philosophers call 'moral agents'. That is, we decide and choose between alternatives on the basis of tradition, revealed truth, personal preference, and so on. From a Christian perspective, we are ultimately responsible to our Maker for the way we live. What AI tempts us to do is to sidestep that responsibility by passing the burden to the machine.

At 4.00 a.m. on 28 March 1979, alarms echoed through number two control room at the Three Mile Island nuclear power plant in Pennsylvania. A tiny valve had stuck, shutting off the secondary cooling system. Seconds later, the uranium core began overheating. People were evacuated from nearby homes. If this had ended in the 'China syndrome', the Pennsylvania countryside (and much besides) would have been covered with radioactivity. The president's commission investigating the near catastrophe noted that engineers had been unable to cope. Why? Information overload. The machines were unmanageable. Human decisions simply made things worse.

If that could have been the end of Pennsylvania as we know it, other errors could have led to the end of the world as we know it. Ballistic missile warning systems, set off by mistake, have almost resulted in the release of nuclear warheads. In one case, the system could not tell a missile from a moonbeam.[17]

In October 1983, the Pentagon issued a 'strategic computing initiative', which proposes to automate critical military decision-making. The hardware development is based on micro-electronics and new systems architecture. The software is AI: expert systems, vision, speech, 'automated reasoning' and natural language understanding. American 'Computer Professionals for Social Responsibility' believe that, far from guaranteeing security, the dangers of automated decision-making are lethal.

They summarize the rationale thus: 'Faster battles push us

to rely more on computers, but current computers can't handle the increased uncertainty and complexity. This means we have to rely on people. But without computer assistance, people can't cope . . . either. So we need new, more powerful computer systems.'[18]

The CPSR report goes on to show how the machines are simply not sufficiently reliable to 'make decisions' of this sort. They may be 'expert' in a specific area, but lack *common sense* (which helps humans distinguish between missiles and moonbeams). Also, the systems are intended for use in crisis situations, precisely when unpredictability is at its greatest. But, in the nature of things, *they cannot be fully tested in advance*. As James Horning of Digital Research Systems, Palo Alto, said of the related Strategic Defense Initiative, one day 'the country will be faced with a cruel dilemma: deploy a system that cannot be trusted, or scrap it'.[19]

We face a huge question. Should we cut ourselves off from that central human capacity: responsibility? In the case of SDI, this problem is built into the proposed technology.

In another case, with less global but no less pressing moral implications, computers are also looked on as solutions. Joseph Fletcher, who in the 1960s made popular the idea of 'situation ethics', argued that the key criterion of moral choice is whether or not it is 'loving'. But how do you *know* when to divorce your husband, or when to tell a white lie is the most loving thing to do?

Fletcher admitted that it is hard to know. But by the 1990s, he declared, things would be much more straightforward. Supercomputers would give us a love calculus for moral choice. Even supposing that this were possible, where does it leave other aspects of moral choice than 'loving rules of thumb'? How would the machine respond to 'I abhor cheating' or 'but we have the mind of Christ'?

I think I have made my point. As a non-participant in technical computer research, I leave the topic with two hopes:
● That such researchers will install adequate 'human windows' in all computer systems, so that people can, as it were, 'see inside'. Expert systems should be built capable of fully

explaining themselves, so that people understand both the computer and their role in relation to it.

● That means of legally certifying new systems will be sought, through public inquiries or equally accountable processes. People's lives, and their quality of life, depend on such systems. In a day when deeper issues are buried in a busy in-tray, some social, ethical test is vital.[20]

Computers could become tyrants, if we let them. Some fears are well founded. Hope lies only in resisting silicon idolatry, and seeing them as tools.

As machines acquire capacities which resemble those of human beings, the issues surrounding the 'machines and persons' connection are pursued with new urgency. Will we sell our moral birthright for a mess of automated pottage? Will we attempt 'to be as God' by creating new beings 'in our own image'?

Let us be clear. Some of the choices I have offered are false ones. Computers are neither exclusively 'friends', nor only 'foes'. Deep ambiguities run through all new technology. Why do I say this? Because if we see computers (or any artifact) as *the* solution to our problems, an entirely friendly and benign development, then we exhibit the first symptoms of silicon idolatry. But if all we see is gigaflop gloom and digital doom, then we are succumbing to the temptation to demonize the machine.

Christians are sojourners in, not natives of the Western world. We should be 'critical watchers' of society, not just 'unreflective participants' in it.[21] So we perceive both faces of new technology, but avoid demonizing or deifying it.

E. F. Schumacher rightly said that deified technology can be summed up as 'a breakthrough a day keeps the crisis at bay'. But he did not spurn technology. Rather, he called for 'appropriate technology'. 'Sojourners' are also what Schumacher calls 'home-comers'. They say 'no' to the 'fads and fascinations of the age', and 'question the presuppositions of a civilization which seems destined to conquer the world'. Like the prodigal, these folk come to their senses, and return home.[22]

But there is a further problem. Have we already advanced too far towards a 'computerized culture'? Is new technology simply cementing the door and bricking up the windows so that we can know no other world?

A computerized culture?

In E. M. Forster's short story, 'The Machine Stops', all the world's inhabitants live underground, each in individual cubicles. All are interconnected, electronically and by utilities channels, providing everything from warm soapy bathwater or piped music to ready-cooked food. The Machine provides for all needs, obviating any human contact — face-to-face and physical — or transport. Progress had been made from previous 'uncivilized' times which were marked by the curious custom of bringing people to things rather than things to people.

Admittedly, when in electronic communication with others the Machine 'did not transmit *nuances* of expression. It only gave a general idea of people — an idea that was good enough for all practical purposes.' But woe betide anyone so timorous as to wish for olden times: 'On atavism the Machine can have no mercy.'[23] The people who made the Machine eventually had to do its bidding, but turned even this into a virtue: 'The word "religion" was sedulously avoided, and in theory the Machine was still the creation and the implement of man. But in practice all, save a few retrogrades, worshipped it as divine.'[24]

Of course, Forster's story is more a reaction against some of H. G. Wells' earlier 'heavens' than a prophetic parable about information technology. Nevertheless, some features — electronic isolation, IT as the Great Provider, and the shaping of human life in the image of the computer — are familiar.

'In technique we trust' could well be the slogan of both Forster's fictional world and ours, although it could not be inscribed on coins in the 'cashless society'. Faith in the technological fix reaches a high point when it extends to solving our political problems (as with SDI). When Forster's Machine stopped, all were destroyed except those who had been banished to the earth's surface as a punishment. It is hard to imagine who would be the beneficiaries of breakdown when the automated military system fails.

The question I want to ask is this. Is the computer shaping our culture, either in subtle or blatant ways? Before dismissing that idea, think of the clock. As Lewis Mumford says, the clock 'is the key machine of the modern industrial age. For every phase of its development the clock is both the outstanding fact and the typical symbol of the machine: even today no other machine is so ubiquitous.'[25] The clock has been called a 'defining technology' because people eat, sleep and work by it. Over time it became a 'necessity' for regulating life, a symbol for precision, which turned punctuality into a virtue.

Plenty of ink has been spilt on the connection between the clock and the Western view of the universe. Even God was seen as a divine clockmaker, constructing an orderly, co-ordinated cosmos. Time became measurable, and had a price put on it: 'time is money.' Is the computer set to become tomorrow's defining technology?

American scholar David Bolter says that by embodying them in a machine, computers make 'new notions of logic, time, space and language accessible and impressive to a vast new audience'.[26] It is the 'principal technological metaphor of our time, chiefly because it can reflect the versatility of the human mind as no previous mechanism could do'.[27]

He asserts that AI is already an 'appropriate technology' because of its aptitude for managing the earth's shrinking resources. Just as once the quest for perpetual motion catalyzed the growth of modern power technology, so he sees AI meeting today's need for careful stewardship. A timely thought. Unfortunately, he seems to have a blind spot when it comes to the main driving force behind AI. It is not stewardship.

That aside, Bolter could have a point. There is no doubt that many people prefer to talk to a computer than with another person. Some students say they prefer electronic devices to teachers, although the evidence suggests that computer-aided learning (CAL) also increases contact *between* pupils. Patients find greater confidentiality in computer diagnosis than the doctor. And pleas are heard for expert systems rather than judges to preside in courtrooms. They think computers will be more impartial.

Joseph Weizenbaum is sceptical. Why does no one ask what's wrong with today's teachers and doctors, or the situations in which they work? What causes them to be rated second best after computers? If we cannot answer this, wheeling in the computer may solve nothing.

But, like it or not, people *do* want more contact with the machine. Computer hobbyists abound, with their attic terminals and their mounds of computing magazines. 'Hacking' seems to be swinging the balance back to participant sport in some places. Serious medical conferences discuss 'computer addiction' among adolescents and others. Having a computer is the indispensable status symbol of any would-be progressive company or school.

Sherry Turkle has explored this 'microworld'. She says that people find all kinds of satisfaction in what she calls the 'subjective computer'. Some are alienated programmers at work. But at home, one speaks of 'a feeling of control when I work in a safe environment of my own creation'. Another, Hannah, says: 'With my computer at home I do everything, I see my whole self, all my kinds of thinking.'

Yet another, Barry, finds a new sense of identity in relation to the machine. Once he thought of himself as being bound by his attitudes and ineptitudes. Now, 'with the computer . . . the deeper you get into it, there's no way an individual can say what he'll be thinking in six months . . . but I honestly feel that it's going to be great.'[28] Turkle hints that although people may 'find themselves' in the computer, they may also lose their feel for 'whole' relationships with other people, and with public life beyond the private or 'in-group' world of the machine. On balance, however, she is optimistic about the computer as a 'second self'.

Well, are computers shaping society and culture? The comparison with clocks, plus some evidence from the 'microworld', seems to suggest that it may be an area to watch. Another angle on the question is this: do computers secularize?

'By the end of the 1980s,' predicts Os Guinness, 'the "mighty micro" will have made its own irrevocable impact on the modern world.' 'Operation gravedigger', the process in which the church digs its own grave, reaches its 'decisive stage' with the invention of the silicon chip.[29]

Michael Shallis offers an explanation for this in *The Silicon Idol*: computers are by definition, 'secular technology'. So far from being extensions of human bodies (like ploughs or bicycles), they recognize 'no gods other than efficiency, progress, and possibly profit and power'.[30]

Make no mistake, secularization is a long-term and para-doxical process.[31] So the answer to 'do computers secularize?' could well be 'yes and no'!

One could agree that more and more of what was once left to God, human initiative, or the forces of nature is 'classified, calculated, or controlled by the use of reason'. Reality is thus contained and constrained by this view of reason (which actually organizes everyday life). And less and less is thought to be beyond the horizon of human experience. We make 'a world without windows'.

Jacques Ellul's view is more focussed. For him, *la technique* is all-powerful, all-pervasive. 'Enclosed within his artificial creation, man finds that there is "no exit"; that he cannot pierce the shell of technology to find again (his) ancient milieu . . .'[32] There can be no 'home-coming'. Back in the 1960s, Ellul foresaw two attempts to control the future. One, to invent 'thinking machines', computers which could mediate between humans and their technical world. Two, to find a new purpose, a new goal for technological society.

The latter, says Ellul, is a false hope. For technique already has a stranglehold. It only allows us to ask 'how?', and not 'why?' questions. *La technique* is an idol whose worshippers are blind to anything beyond it. Who needs 'You shall not steal' when bar codes in books prevent them leaving the library unstamped? Who needs another justification for SDI than that it appears to offer a technological solution to the cold war?

The problem here is that Ellul seems to explain *everything* as dominated by technique. It appears that by definition the signs of hope (to which I have tried to point) are illusions. The same criticism may be made against the 'strong' version of secularization. Is it really an unstoppable force, squeezing all society and culture into a rational mould?

As to the artifacts themselves being secular, I have doubts. Some regard computing as a 'craft' technology. And the idea that craft technologies were 'sacred' is just romantic nostalgia. They too could serve idols.

I am sure that a 'computer mentality' does help obscure the relevance of 'value' questions, just as, in a related field, changing communications affect the way we see the world. Writing helped bind people together round common beliefs and traditions. Electronic communications sometimes erode tradition by encouraging an 'instant' and 'artificial' view of the world.

On the other hand, the emergence of 'computer Bible schools' in North America, or the 'Church Computer Users' Group' in Britain suggests that some are quick to exploit the potential of new technology in the *service* of traditional religion. Who can tell what will be the eventual outcome of these apparently countervailing trends?

Computers do nothing to help reverse secular trends, and thus probably contribute to the 'world without windows'. But they do this not because they are inherently evil, but because of the world-views, the human purposes and interests, with which they are suffused. *La technique* is truly an idol. But idols lack power.

We have seen how new technology may help perpetuate one already existing tendency. We finish our survey of 'the computerized culture' by asking if this is true of another trait of our society: male domination.

Victorian Charles Babbage was a founding father of computing. If his analytical engine had really worked, then his friend, Ada Countess Lovelace (Lord Byron's daughter) could justly have claimed to be the world's first programmer. But for all the women in programming today, very few actually hold positions of real responsibility in the high-tech world. As with cars, women often appear in computer advertisements in poses which have no connection with computer *use*.[33] Boys are hooked on computer games and monopolize the school machines. Some even say that men tend to think in a more computer-like *algorithmic* fashion, whereas women think *analogically*. So the title of one book about 'living and growing with computers' is no accident. It is *Microman*.[34]

Much technology is male-oriented, but does it have to be so? Arnold Pacey contrasts the heroic Greek artisan-god Hephaistos — who provides the more influential model — with the goddess Pallas Athene, noted for intellectual and moral qualities of her practical work, and for meticulous craft skill.[35] He adds that Homer's contemporary, writing the biblical book of Proverbs, ended with poetic praise for the caring, wise, industrious craftswoman and estate manager.

Today, technology's 'expert' angle, focussing either on economic or technical matters, is predominantly male. But what of the 'user' or 'need-oriented' angle? Women experience technology less in terms of making things (the 'expert') than of managing processes (such as conserving, nourishing and growing). Women could have a very positive role in technology, if only they had the chance. They could help curb the 'dominating' approach (affecting both 'nature' and other persons) which so frequently takes technology well beyond properly human bounds.[36]

If this critique has any validity (as I think it has) then computers are certainly not closing this social divide between the sexes. There is no intrinsic reason why computing should be a 'male technology'. I believe it should not be.

In the biblical view, the opening up of creation's latent potential — using different technologies — is a task given to *human beings*, not males only. There is a strong case for male/female *partnership* in technology. In fact, to foster that partnership is one of the most significant ways of reorienting technology. Greater conformity to divine directives in this and other areas opens the door to technology shaped for human needs, rather than mere technical or economic 'imperatives'.

From information to wisdom

How did we reach the point at which technical solutions are offered for political problems, as in the case of the 'Star Wars' programme? And what led us to entertain thoughts of the technical solutions being partly independent of our decisions, as in the case of the 'automated battlefield'? The answer is silicon idolatry. For once we *believe in* the technology, its wider context and consequences escape us. After that, we see more technology as the only answer. Idols blind us and idols bind us, remember?

Joseph Weizenbaum neatly distils the point: people have failed to distinguish between 'information, knowledge and wisdom, between calculating, reasoning, and thinking, and finally . . . between a society centred on human beings and one centred on machines'.[37] Quite so.

But biblical thought takes us further. Talk of a humane society always carries the risk of concluding (with Alexander Pope) that 'the measure of mankind is man'. Not a feminist complaint about language this time, but a reminder that the 'measure' of humanness is that we are the 'image of God'. So what does this require of us?

That enigmatic old-time sage Ecclesiastes made it perfectly clear. Respect for God is the root of wisdom. And the wise person follows God's ways for human life. Worse than fools, warns the proverb, are people wise in their own eyes.

All of this makes the idea of computers as a 'defining technology' appear rather trivial. To see ourselves as 'information processors made of meat' we have to be looking through the wrong end of the telescope. No, we cannot move from information to wisdom, but we can move the other way. For wisdom, that practical knowledge which is a divine gift, provides a proper perspective on new technology. We may get it in focus, in context.

A few years ago, launching the British 'Micro-electronic Education Programme', Prime Minister Thatcher referred to the 'keyboard generation'. New skills were sought to make young people 'computer literate', ready for jobs of the 'information age'. The youngest children, urges a recent report, should know about technology.[38] This seems fair enough on the surface. But where does wisdom come in? Here are a couple of questions:

● What will happen as education spending is *shifted* from other areas? Some fear that children will grow up imagining that the only *significant* information is the kind that can be stripped from a text, stored on a database, and retrieved. What of narrative, fiction, poetry, and the spiritual dimensions of life?[39]

John Maddison, in *Education in the Microelectronics Era*, cautions that the spirit of Dickens' Gradgrind ('facts, nothing but the facts') is still at large. The 'hydraulic theory of education', which likens children to vessels, and teachers to liquid-pourers, gets a boost from IT. New technology can 'inundate the student with a flood of visual and auditory stimuli, literally filling every channel, inlet, passage, and canal leading to the student's brain'.[40]

● What *sort* of thing should children know about new technology? Well, 'hands-on' keyboard skills, an understanding of databases, and something about real-life applications. And what else? The answer is, precious little. A syllabus in computer studies has been likened to one on swimming pools, covering pools from ancient Rome to the present, pool architecture, construction and water-chemistry, and so on. Swimming and paddling not included.[41] This means that *la technique* rules the schools as well.

In the UK (which has been accepted by other countries as a model of micro-electronics education) two things are happening. One is a 'sign of hope'. The MEP acknowledges that the wider context of society and ethics should be part of 'IT awareness'.[42] I know not how to describe the other. But the MEP is closing shop, with only a slimline, if not skinny, replacement.

So we may be left listening to voices crying in the wilderness, after all. Let us hear them, loud and clear! As Mike Parsons points out, many of the taught skills are quickly becoming irrelevant as machines are more user-friendly. It is questions about security, data flow, responsibility, decision-making which really count as 'computer awareness'. Let us be sure that people learn what computers *can not* as well as what they *can* do.[41]

But this should not be limited to high school classrooms! Computer awareness of this sort should be on the educational agenda in the very broadest sense. Community groups, churches, TV programmes, firms and families should know what is happening all around us. Silicon idolatry seeps everywhere, throwing up smokescreens to obscure the real issues of the day. Only the wise will perceive them.

I do not say, however, that education is a cure for idolatry! It can easily become an idol in its own right. This thought takes me back to the Hebrews. They were liberated from the slave economy of ancient Egypt. They also escaped entanglement in Egypt's futile idolatry, their worship of the Nile and the sacred beetle, which helped shape their culture and society. They could not liberate themselves. Only YHWH, their God, could mount the rescue.

Knowing their weakness, YHWH warned that any regression to idols would have dire consequences, lasting to the third and fourth generation. If, on the other hand, they loved him, and lived by his wisdom, he would show love to them. Their liberated life meant a caring community, stable families, economically fair and ecologically sound practices — even in technology.

Centuries later, we are moving from the fourth to the fifth generation of computers. Perhaps this play on words can act as a timely reminder of the long-term consequences of today's developments. Egypt's beetles and Canaan's baals were helpless to liberate. So is the silicon idol. But with wisdom as guide, could the 'mighty micro' not be shaped for a liberated life? Who will face the challenge of this fearfully ambiguous 'fifth generation'?

Notes

1 *The Guardian*, 12 November 1985

2 *The Sunday Times*, 10 February 1985

3 Unpublished report of the Research Institute for Consumer Affairs, quoted in Shirley Williams, *A Job to Live*, Penguin, 1985, page 89

4 These examples come from Laurie Taylor, 'Have you met my machine?', *The Times*, 3 June 1985

5 Os Guinness, *The Gravedigger File*, Hodder and Stoughton, 1983, page 61

6 William Marbach, 'The race to build a supercomputer' in Tom Forester (ed.) *The Information Technology Revolution*, Blackwell, 1985, page 60

7 Margaret Boden, quoted in Michael Shallis, *The Silicon Idol*, Oxford University Press, 1984, page 154

8 Edward Feigenbaum and Pamela McCorduck, *The Fifth Generation*, Pan, 1984

9 Donald Michie, in Trevor Jones, *Microelectronics and Society*, Open University Press, 1980, page 115

10 Donald Michie and Rory Johnston, *The Creative Computer*, Penguin, 1985, page 34

11 Joseph Weizenbaum, *Computer Power and Human Reason*, Penguin, 1984

12 Donald MacKay, *Brains, Machines and Persons*, Eerdmans/Collins, 1980, page 64. See also Gordon Clarke, 'Does AI threaten genuine faith?' in *Faith and Thought*, 1982, 109, 1

13 Clifton Orlebeke, 'The behaviour of robots' in Clifton Orlebeke and Lewis Smedes (eds) *God and the Good*, Eerdmans, 1975, page 219

14 *Newsweek*, 4 July 1983

15 *The Guardian*, 1 August 1985

16 Alan Jiggins, 'A world without windows', *Third Way*, January 1985, pages 10–13

17 See *Computing and Social Responsibility*, 1985, a set of discussion papers from the Society, Religion and Technology Project (available from the Church of Scotland, 121 George Street, Edinburgh, UK)

18 See note 17

19 *The Guardian*, 7 November 1985

20 Egbert Schuurman, *The Threatening Tension in the Technological Society* (forthcoming)

21 Mary Van Leeuwen, *The Person in Psychology: a Contemporary Christian Appraisal*, IFACS and Eerdmans, 1985

22 E. F. Schumacher, *Small is Beautiful*, Abacus, 1973

23 E. M. Forster, 'The Machine Stops' in *The Collected Works of E. M. Forster*, Sidgwick and Jackson, 1948, pages 118, 137

24 E. M. Forster (see above), page 147

25 Lewis Mumford, *Technics and Civilization*, Harcourt, Brace, 1934, page 14

26 David Bolter, *Turing's Man: Western Culture in the Computer Age*, Duckworth, 1984, page 33

27 David Bolter (see above), page 40

28 Sherry Turkle, 'The subjective computer' in *Social Studies of Science*, 1982, 12, pages 173–205

29 Os Guinness, *The Gravedigger File*, Hodder and Stoughton, 1983, page 17

30 Michael Shallis, *The Silicon Idol*, Oxford University Press, 1984, page 93

31 David Lyon, *The Steeple's Shadow: the Myths and Realities of Secularization*, SPCK, 1985

32 Jacques Ellul, *The Technological Society*, London: Cape, 1964; New York: Vintage, page 428

33 Mike Cooley, *Architect or Bee?*, Langley Technical Services, 1980, pages 42–44

34 Gordon Pask and Susan Curran, *Microman*, Century Publishing, 1982

35 Arnold Pacey, *The Culture of Technology*, Blackwell, 1983, page 97

36 Paul Tournier, *The Gift of Feelings*, SCM Press, 1981

37 Joseph Weizenbaum, 'The myths of artificial intelligence' in Tom Forester (ed.) *The Information Technology Revolution*, Blackwell, 1985, page 24

38 HMI discussion document, *The Curriculum 5–16*, reported in *The Times*, 14 March 1985

39 Gwen Gawith, 'What price information?', *Education Librarians' Bulletin*, 1984, 27, 2, pages 38–42

40 John Maddison, *Education in a Microelectronics Era*, Open University Press, 1983, page 27

41 Michael Parsons, 'The religious meaning of the microcomputer', *The Guardian*, 3 October 1985

42 *Microelectronics Education Programme: The Strategy*, London, 1981. See also MEP, *All Change: the Consequences of Automation and IT for Secondary Education*, National Extension College, 1984 (especially the section by the British Computer Society)

5
The 'information age': threats and promises

He only popped out to do some evening shopping at the grocery store. As he turned into the car park he became aware of the flashing lights of a police car behind him. He had made an illegal left turn.

Michael Ducross, a gentle Canadian-born Indian, waited while the policeman checked with the local station over his two-way radio. The clerk (in Huntington, California) keyed the details into his computer, flashing a request for information to Sacramento. Nothing showed up. 3,000 miles away, however, in Washington's National Crime Information Center, the FBI's computerized records showed that Michael Ducross had gone absent without leave from the Marine Corps — ten years before.

For the next five months, Ducross was detained at the Marine Corps' Camp, Pendleton. On his release, when all charges were dropped, he explained that the government had discovered the truth. Never absent without leave, he had in fact obtained discharge under a special programme for foreign citizens and native Americans. I do not know what happened to his groceries.[1]

A village shop was the scene of another police data incident, this time in England. A policeman's wife happened to overhear some malicious gossip to the effect that a man she knew by name was a potential paedophile. Somehow that name found its way onto the police computer, where it remained until the day he applied for a job. A personnel intelligence company, engaged to look into the background of job candidates, unearthed the computer file. Someone else got the job.[2]

Of all the threats associated with the 'information age', violations of personal privacy seem the most sinister. Someone somewhere knows all about me through my driving record, my credit cards, my employment details, and so on. 'Big Brother' no longer appears as a fictional character. Information technology makes possible government and police surveillance on a scale that even George Orwell might have found hard to imagine.

But is the overall picture so flagitious? Do we not simply have to trade off with the threats the benefits of sophisticated crime detection, easy payment of bills, and more efficient bureaucracies? After all, no one could actually *want* to repeat the delays in catching the 'Yorkshire Ripper', which were attributed in part to the clumsy index-card system. Surely no one *likes* to weigh down, and wear out, their pockets with cash every time they go shopping? And obtaining correct and quick welfare payments from a computerized system is definitely preferable to the long line, the stigma of discussing personal details, and the uncertain wait for satisfaction.

I am not sure that things are so simple. In this chapter we explore some of the reasons why. Potential technological promise is real enough. But lingering doubts are equally real, and refuse to go away just because someone produces a plausible reason for introducing IT.

What we must remember is that the quest of new technology is part of a wider pattern of events. Why are we installing information systems at all? What vision of the future guides our decisions? Or do we have no 'vision'? Are we just working on the assumption that more technology means a better life?

Some of our visionaries are well placed to influence the future. For instance, Britain's pioneer of small computers, Sir Clive Sinclair, foresees computer equivalents to the human brain within ten or twenty years. The difference between the new Golden Age and Periclean Athens is that robots, not slaves, will take charge of all production. Beyond that, he says, is the age of space cities, the search for worlds beyond the solar system, and the colonization of the galaxy.[3]

It may seem small-minded, but others, with different visions, would prefer not to inhabit Sir Clive's electronic

Eden. Typesetters strike against job losses, civil libertarians protest against privacy invasion, internationalists complain about coca-colonization by satellite and despair for the deepening divide between information-rich and poor. Others fear for the future of all-round education or resist the reductionism which sees humans as machines. In short, their reception of IT is a lot more cautious.

Our first task is to raise questions about security. Is the 'information age' a threat because of hackers, Big Brother, or for more subtle reasons? Second, we explore the 'techno-freaks' and 'technophobes' phenomena more closely. What are their background beliefs? How do their ideas work out in real life, in policies and strategies?

Third, we return to another recurrent theme: how should *we* respond? Some decisive choices (about computers and cable) have already been made. Already we are creating a society dependent upon IT which in many respects is deeply different from what we now know. Is it realistic to try to put the clock back? Or rather does realism demand responsibility? And where would this take us?

If so, what about the wrong turnings already taken? What of our commitment to human technical creativity, our realism about the consequences of distorted vision and practice in personal and social life, our dependence on wisdom from beyond the human horizon, and our search for signs of hope? Can there be responsible technology? Do opportunities exist to salt the earth, to light the world?

Computer state or computer democracy?

Did your grandparents have driver's licences, social security numbers, credit cards, high school and college registration, a payroll and a tax code? It is highly unlikely that more was publicly recorded about them than that they were born, married, had children, and died.

We now inhabit another world. Huge computerized databases contain a mass of basic information about each one of us. But not only that. Computers generate what is called 'transactional information', about phone calls, bills paid, and so on. What do you think is happening when your credit card number is read into a phone before you make a big purchase? Who else knows the state of your account? And how many others will know similar information when you start shopping and banking by two-way cable?

It doesn't stop there either. Information can be shifted at great speed over vast distances. Think of poor Michael Ducross! Databases can also 'talk' with each other, and do! David Burnham, in *The Rise of the Computer State*, cites the case of Billy Carter, brother of the former US president.

Working with the American Telephone and Telegraph Company (AT&T), the FBI found evidence for the Democratic Senate Committee investigating Carter's connection with Libya. On 26 November 1979, Billy Carter and friend began driving from Washington to Georgia. At 3.43 a five-minute call to the Libyan embassy was charged to Carter's number from Jonesboro, an Atlanta suburb. Many other calls were similarly footnoted. The data had been obtained legally (though this is not always so).[4]

American government officials have over 4,000 million separate records on US citizens. An internal communications network serving just one multinational corporation links more than 500 computers in over a hundred cities in at least eighteen different countries. 10,000 merchants all over the US can obtain a summary fact sheet on any one of 86 million American citizens in three or four seconds from a single database in southern California.[5]

Did you know that in Britain the police national computer holds 5 million entries under the criminal names index? But it also has access, if necessary, to other files. Two government departments alone (Home Office and Department of Health and Social Security) hold 113 million detailed personal records. Any person in Britain who owns a car has his or her name with the PNC, along with 32.8 million others. Another source, of interest to the PNC, is the National TV Licence Records Office, whose machine contains 18.6 million entries.[6]

All this raises questions, as well as eyebrows. Those in Britain concerned for civil liberties insist that three matters be faced. First is secrecy. Information may be held without the individual's full knowledge. Second, as in our first examples, the information may be wrong, or outdated. Third — and here's a paradox — the 'confidential' information may only be hidden from that particular person's eyes. Others have access to it.[7]

Britain lags behind other countries in data legislation. The 1984 Data Protection Act is a belated step forward, spurred by Britain's being out of line with the rest of Europe. Most collectors of data now have to register. People who think someone holds data on them have a right to check it. But the spirit of the Act is only 'data protection', not 'freedom of information' which Americans have.

So even assuming someone in Britain had the suspicion, was motivated to investigate, and could pay the possible fee, they may not actually see what they want to. There is little to stop data holders programming their machines to divulge only *part* of the record. What is worse, no government control exists on the *quality* of information held. Gossip about paedophiles may evade scrutiny.

Many look to highly-computerized Sweden for guidance. When Stig Bjerstrom filed his income tax return one February, he claimed back 1,000 kronor. The tax office sent him two computer notices. One said he would get back 800 kronor. The other warned that if he failed to send the 8,000 kronor he *owed*, they would start deducting it from his salary.

Justly angry, Bjerstrom appealed to the Data Inspection Board, which Swedes have had since 1973. The Board checked the records, found them in error, and asked the tax office to correct them. But tax office records now showed Bjerstrom was dead. (Others thought so, too, because his wife received junk 'sympathy' mail, including an offer of a cut-price hot water bottle for cold winter nights.) Data Inspection Director, Jan Freese, decided it was time for human intervention, and Bjerstrom — alive and well — got his money.[8]

Respect and protection for the individual has long been a duty supported by Christian churches in the West. With the rapid spread of new means of electronic surveillance, efforts

should be redoubled to secure people from Big Brother's prying eyes. We are not up against a conspiracy, so much as
technologies which grow faster than we can regulate their use.
The example of Sweden, which for instance also monitors
'gates' between different databases, is worth watching.

To return to computers used in the legal process; if we
believe in forgiveness, we will want to see even this embodied
in new technology. Should we not clear computer records of
crimes after good behaviour? In the USA, even after acquit-
tal, 'criminal' records may still be kept.[9] This is a blatant denial
of principles (which surely have Christian support?) about
'restoring' and 'rehabilitating' the innocent and the reformed.

New technology does not itself determine the direction we
go. But as it multiplies, it constrains our choices. And the
more we feel our choices to be constrained, the more we feel
tempted to fall back on technical solutions for the problems of
the system in question. Yet even those 'technical solutions' are
pregnant with ethical implication. The issue is how to find and
apply proper ethical standards to pressing problems.

Yes, at least from a technical point of view the 'computer
state' is nearer than when Orwell wrote *1984*. However, this is
to ignore factors which, others say, is the opposite of that
sinister scenario. Could IT open the door to a new 'computer
democracy'?

We are already aware of the mighty power of direct mail,
especially in American elections. Computerized letters appeal
person-to-person for support. Groups can be 'targeted' in
other ways, too, for instance using computers to dial people's
phones and relay taped messages. But the main hope for
'push-button politics' resides in cable TV.

The cable system in Reading, Pennsylvania, was among the
first to provide live coverage of city council meetings. Karen
Miller, who was elected mayor after this, put down her victory
over the political machine to the following attracted by this
local political TV show.[9] Again, cable offers the potential to
speak directly to interest groups, a far cry from the blunder-
buss approach of party political broadcasts.

Even more dramatic is the possibility of electronic polling.

The Qube experiment in Columbus, Ohio, included trials of an 'instant referendum' type. (Just think of the silly and serious possibilities: Do you favour green or blue tiles in the Anglo-French channel tunnel? Should hijackers be hung, yes or no?) Alvin Toffler sees electronic polling as part of the new participatory politics of the *Third Wave*. But will push-button politics really work?

Unfortunately for enthusiasts, the answer must be 'no'. For a start, only those with the right equipment are involved, so it would be participation for the urban, better-off citizen. Then, there is no way of telling *who* is pushing the buttons. Our two-year-old daughter, Miriam, loves to adjust the TV set and to play with keyboards . . .! Also, the instant referendum would invite abuse by emotional appeal. Rational choice would be minimal. Lastly, it would let politicians off the hook as far as making hard decisions is concerned.

Again, this example shows the seductive appeal of technological solutions for political and social problems. The shadow of the silicon idol falls across our path once more. But even if push-button politics is an inadequate counterweight to the computer state, IT *is* likely to have repercussions for the political process. The balance of power — especially in the USA — could tilt more towards interest groups, and away from traditional parties.

One way of providing greater access to information (such as government policy discussions and statements) would be to establish *public* databases. IT could in this way function like early newspapers did in promoting an informed democracy, but at present such ideas receive little consideration. Potential does exist for creating a more democratic society, using IT. But where is the will for it to be realized?

Hackers and history

'I was a teenage hacker' is the kind of true-life confession making headlines in the 1980s. 'Hackers' are the people who break into computer systems, who crack codes, and use others' passwords. It may only involve cheeky messages, like the one sent to Prince Philip using his personal Prestel code.

Or it may be high school children finding an electronic route into the Pentagon.

High-tech robbery is a major new form of criminal activity, of which hacking is only one variety. A dentist was jailed for eighteen months in 1983 for submitting 8,462 false claims to the British Dental Estimates Board ICL computer. He netted over £300,000 this way. Fortunately, another computer threw up his name as the wealthiest British dentist! Others transfer money from bank accounts, or take advantage of 'bugs' in the computer programs. In the USA, the Stanford Research Institute reckons that computer fraud accounts for over $4.5 thousand million, while in the UK, figures range between £500 million and £2.5 thousand million per year.[10]

Computer crime is expanding. The more new electronic lines are opened, and remote terminals established, the greater will be the opportunities. Of course, those defrauded or broken into are getting wiser, and computer security is rapidly becoming an industry in its own right.

I mention computer crime here, not because I have any 'solutions' to offer, but rather to draw attention to a weightier matter. We are creating a fragile framework for society. Without inflating the importance of 'data', we might say that the very category of 'truth' becomes more questionable.

A society infused with IT is highly vulnerable. The sheer size and complexity of computerized information systems tends to make them humanly unmanageable. A confidential report (how do I know?) apparently warns that the British government should decentralize its computers to prevent unions gaining a stranglehold on vital Whitehall operations.[11]

But it is not just political vulnerability. Of course prudence demands that safeguards and security be built into computer systems. The social framework becomes frail and fragile the more we simply substitute technical control for moral constraint. The culture which sneeringly discards the old virtues — such as truth — simultaneously snatches at anything available to shore up the edifice once supported by them.

Perhaps bigger issues lurk here than at first meet the eye.

For just as 'information' becomes more central to the functioning of society, the means of destroying, altering or losing it also becomes more available. For those who speak the language of 'truth' and 'lies', the 'information age' acquires a more serious mien.

Paradoxically, the study of history could be more difficult in the 'information age'. William King, archivist at Duke University, North Carolina, fears that the rapid pace of change in computers could leave heaps of magnetic discs and tapes unreadable to future historians. They will simply lack the means to gain access to the data![12]

As well as being trapped by obsolete technology, information may also be 'zapped' by today's technology. Here lies a key concern for the so-called 'information age'. Many ethical questions which confront us in information technology are old ones in new guise. Their long-term and global dimensions add to their complexity, but in themselves they are not new. The malleability of data — the fact that information may be irretrievably and invisibly erased, or 'zapped' — is a novel issue.

Hackers depend on it when they try to cover their tracks, as did the Pentagon when it allowed its computers to 'lie' about who was really being bombed during the Vietnam war (it was Cambodia).[13] Orwell's fictional police state deliberately altered records and 'changed history'. In real life the Soviet Union has done the same, by removing Trotsky from photographic records of the 1920s, for instance. But they used clumsy and detectable methods. Today's digital retouching of photos and erasure of data is extremely hard to discover. No tourist could guess from the travel brochure that the hotel lawn is in reality a car park.

The potential for the distortion of the truth is daily augmented as new information systems are set up. Paradoxically, the 'information age' holds no guarantees that we will 'know' any more. It was no authoritarian dictatorship which tried to prevent the publication of the Pentagon Papers, authorized extensive phone-tapping of real and imagined enemies, and persuaded TV networks to defuse opposition to Richard

Nixon's public speeches. And it is not only in Eastern Europe that TV documentaries are censored before broadcasting.

If such events can occur in the familiar world of television and telephones, should we not be ready for repeat performances — only more sophisticated and with greater consequence — in the 'information age'? The 'readiness' I have in mind is two-edged. One, let us support the search for appropriate safeguards. Two, and more fundamentally, let us practise truth in every level of life.

Toward an electronic Eden?

Britain declared 1982 'Information Technology Year'. Kenneth Baker, then minister for IT, set the scene: 'The age of information technology . . . has arrived. I know of no other technological advance which has brought together so many areas of rapid and exciting development. Computers and telecommunications are converging very rapidly, huge investments are being made, and the impact of IT will be felt at every level of our society . . .'[14]

The big question is, 'why?'. Did the 'information age' arrive like the morning mail? Are the technologies 'converging' all by themselves, like the proverbial couple on the ballroom balcony? We have argued against such ideas. Technology is a *human* construction. We can trace its origins, uncover the interests it serves. Let us review four elements within that 'human construction', four reasons for 'going informatic':

● **'Automate or liquidate.'** Warding off economic decline tops national, as well as company agendas. For the latter, keeping a market share, and reducing costs, is crucial. At the national level, a Canadian government publication admits: 'In the quest for survival that is sweeping a very competitive world, economic policy has become technology policy.'[15] Of course, to recognize this is one thing. The *kind* of technology policy adopted is another.

In Britain and the USA, allowing enterprise free rein (whether by 'privatizing' or 'deregulating' companies), plus giving research incentives, is the chosen route. Other countries, notably France and Japan, adopt a more *dirigiste* approach. Many home computers have been installed free of charge in France. Experimental 'wired cities' are being established, for example in Lille and Biarritz. Japan, whose highly confident Ministry of Industry and International Trade (MIIT) co-ordinates its plan, is busy building fourteen new 'technopolises' to reduce urban overcrowding and to maintain a leading edge in new technology.[16]

Whether 'information society' plans will really succeed outside Japan is open to question. For other forces are also at work, including our second reason for 'going informatic'.

● **'Information is power.'** The French and Japanese IT initiatives have been less dependent on 'defence' funding. But the Americans (especially) see the 'fifth generation' project in terms of its *political* potential. The US Defense Department is the single largest user of telecommunications. The Pentagon telecommunications budget is roughly the size of all revenues taken by *all* TV and radio stations in the USA.[17] Britain's big electronics companies — Plessey, Ferranti, GEC — scooped by far the biggest share of the 1985 £7.1 billion defence equipment budget.[18]

IT is not innocent in the arms race. For many countries, micro-electronics and defence are inseparably linked. And 'information is power' has other faces as well. Within individual countries, IT may be used for state surveillance. 'Silicon society' will not necessarily be safe.

● **'Information is control.'** For the companies, as distinct from the countries who wish to 'go informatic', this is a major factor. In most general terms, IT helps people organize human life.

We may transmit information faster, design a bridge more accurately, and so on. Singapore hopes to relieve urban congestion by using sensors under the road to levy tolls on motorists. And Franco Benedetti of Olivetti hopes to relieve some management headaches: 'IT is basically a technology of control and co-ordination of the labour force.'[19] (There are two ways of reading that, however.)

● **The bandwagon effect.** Everybody is computerizing; join the quest for keyboard kudos! Many advertisements play subtly on the theme of prestige. They hint that to delay in the IT revolution is to side with *ancien regime*. Who wants to be left in the Stone Age — or even the paper age? Research in California shows that people fall for it: 'To be modern and up-to-date in the 1980s is to computerize. This has symbolic as well as instrumental value for individuals and organizations who want to present a progressive and forward-looking image.'[20]

Needless to say, this simply begs other questions. Why is it so important to appear 'progressive'? After all, other cultures put value on being like your ancestors, or keeping the traditions of the *past*. Why is adopting 'tomorrow's technology' such a big deal? To answer this we must dig deeper. We have to go beneath the explicit reasons, to uncover beliefs buried just below the surface. These taken-for-granted ideas also impel us into the 'information age'.

'Progress' is one of the most deeply-held beliefs of the Western world (and one which has successfully been exported everywhere). Whether through potent symbols such as clocks or calculators, electric or nuclear power, or through steadily rising graph-curves of performance improvement, progress is seen as a 'visible fact' of modernity. The conviction that human beings could actively and independently remake a better world helped catapult us into the capitalist, industrial era.[21] The same conviction inspires immortal lines such as 'Silicon Valley holds the keys to the kingdom.'

Somehow belief in progress survives other 'visible facts' such as increased energy consumption on mechanized farms, radioactive risk from nuclear waste, and the artificial pacing of life by the clock. It also survives the impact of war and recession, although it may now have one or two 'government health warnings' attached.

For instance, progress is no longer the *inevitable* result of technological innovation as it appeared in the 1960s. Success in the global contest for market shares, and popular development of innovations is required to avoid *regress* to 'Third

World status'. But that is only a negative appeal to the same belief. No, progress is not yet dead, and the microchip wonder-drug has done a lot to revive it.

Belief in technological progress is not wrong because it stimulates discovery, innovation, and improvement. It is wrong both because technology is lifted out of the realm of human decisions and social context, and because it is then accorded a 'life of its own'.

How often are we told, 'It's progress; you can't stop it'? But this is misleading. True, many choices we make cannot be *reversed*, but they are still *choices*. And research programmes can be halted, tree-and-branch cable systems can be upgraded to switched star, and computerized machines can be used to co-operate with, not replace human skill.

Jacques Ellul attacks the way that technology is allowed to take its own course, guided only by technical or economic criteria.[22] He says the only 'ethic' known by the technological outlook is 'correct practice' (not motive or intention), and that it tends to rule out traditional ethics (which recognize the ambiguity of real life). Don't forget, though, that technology *does* exhibit 'ethical' stances. So the task is not so much to 're-inject' ethics into technology, as to recognize those quasi-ethics which are in fact operating, and to offer alternative, explicit and more adequate guidelines.

This is why we hear so frequently, and with a shrug, 'But we have no choice.' No technical choice, or no economic choice; these two are cousins. 'No technical choice' is illustrated from history. The spinning-jenny, the steam engine, and the car were the 'only logical developments'. Feigenbaum and McCorduck see history repeating itself. Just as Henry Ford was bound to come along sooner or later to mass produce what the Benz Patent Motor Wagon makers crafted so carefully, so the Japanese will mass produce their 'fifth generation' for the waiting world of the 1990s.

'No economic choice' appears starkly in the 'automate or liquidate' slogan. New inventions offering economic reward are developed. Those which can be marketed competitively succeed, others fall by the wayside. In this blinkered view, socially-useful or more durable products, or different work-organization, are excluded from sight.

But economic disaster need not follow just because we take the blinkers off. Lord Shaftesbury's famous 'Ten Hours Act' of 1847, which restricted child labour in English factories, is a good example. Its opponents warned that continuous reduction in hours would ruin British industry. In Cobbett's words the riches of England were discovered to be 'all nothing worth compared with the labour of three thousand little girls in Lancashire . . . from whose labour, if we deduct only two hours a day, away goes the wealth . . . the capital . . . the resources, the power, and the glory of England'![23]

'No economic choice' may not blind people only to the alternatives available for products and work situations. It may also blind them to the long-term consequences of today's decisions. Will some cable companies regret their early start, whose promise of short-term profit prevented them from installing systems which realize cable's fuller potential?

Despite the halo of high-tech hype, then, the 'information age' does not exactly appear as an 'electronic Eden'. Perhaps we would do better to turn our backs on it and join the 'computer Canutes'?

Computer Canutes?

The symptoms of technophobia spring up all over the place. The Toronto *Globe and Mail* carried an article in mid-1984 with the engaging title: 'The awful price of the computer age.' Word processors are job-killers and writers' crutches, psychologist B. F. Skinner's advocacy of teaching machines is the prelude to behaviour control under the guise of education, video-games produce stupid, sullen, and hyper-active children, personal computers make possible the more rapid and absolute accomplishment of things that should not be done or 'are not worth doing', and so on.[24]

Some British sixteen to eighteen-year-old students told researchers that they didn't believe in the high-tech future. They expect tomorrow to be rather like today, with more violence, boredom, unemployment, and inflation. Few are excited by the 'super-industrial materialist future that politicians of all parties assume we all want'.[25]

Of course, it would be easy to dismiss these as the jaundiced views of the ignorant. On returning from Russia in the 1930s, Beatrice Webb is supposed to have said: 'I have seen the future, and it works.' What of those who have already seen the IT future? Does *it* work? News from Silicon Valley itself is mixed. On the one hand are those who claim to have found new, relaxed work-styles, and the decline of old worker-boss distinctions.

On the other hand, people report incredibly pressured lives, and high-level stress within spiralling career patterns. The prizes may be glittering, but the price, in some cases, is ghastly. The more people are committed to the high-tech project, the less they can rely on family and community support. The competition, the long hours, the intensity of work, the size of the risks, all make life precarious. Marriages dissolve. Job-loss is just as devastating. They call it 'Silicon Valley Fever'. If these are the 'industries of the future', beware![26]

Little wonder, then, that 'computer Canutes' arise. They want to hold back the technological tide. They remember 3 June 1980, when American pilots boarded their B-52 bombers ready to repel the Russian nuclear attack — alerted by computers. They see their craft skills as newspaper type-setters disappearing into the journalists' keyboard; bypassed by computer. They swear they will never buy cable TV for fear of Big Brother. The more usual pejorative term for them is 'Luddites'.

But some today deliberately adopt a 'Luddite' stance, and take pride in so doing. Why? The original Luddites, who took their name from their legendary leader, Ned Ludd, felt overwhelmed by the early industrial revolution. They system-atically smashed stocking frames in Nottinghamshire, England, in the 1830s. Only *some* stocking frames were broken though, the ones they identified as contributing to lower wages or loss of skills.

Luddism, which quickly grew into a movement, was based partly on social class. Behind that lay complex cultural and social changes. Although many rejoiced to see feudal master-servant relationships removed, others felt the loss. Buffers against poverty *had been* provided in the religiously sanctioned duty of masters to men. Workers' welfare was not in their hands alone. As R. H. Tawney observes, Luddism was also a response to the 'secularization of political thought'. Property and profit increasingly came before people. With the pay packet as the only surviving link between employer and employed, workers justly felt vulnerable.[27]

Today's revived Luddism generally remembers only half the Luddite story. The class association is kept but the question of religion and ethics is left on one side. Its value lies in destroying the 'frenzied bigot' view of Luddism, and in asserting that all technical change is also *social* change. But unless one wishes to explain all new technology by its role in the contest between 'capital' and 'labour', neo-Luddism will be seen as limited in both theory and practice.[28]

Another response, seen sometimes, but less deservedly, as that of the 'computer Canute', springs from a more 'ecological' critique. The wasteful, pollutive, and exploitative aspects of twentieth-century technology prompt a growing number of people to seek alternatives. Their most prominent mentor is Fritz Schumacher, who pioneered the quest of 'appropriate technology' for the Third World. In the phrase 'small is beautiful' we hear how it also applies to the 'advanced' societies.

This is not a 'back to nature' drive, which revels in Welsh hillside teepee villages or in tilling virgin soil in the Australian outback. Nor is it rightly equated with the romanticized life-style of technology-resisting groups such as the North American Old Order Mennonites or Amish. (They drive horse-drawn buggies and practise largely unmechanized farming.) I am not thinking of those who *reject* technology as a reaction; rather, of those trying to promote *realistic* alternatives.

In 1975 a committee (representing 13,000 workers) at Lucas Aerospace, England, proposed a plan for 'useful' technology. The idea was to offset recession and redundancy. Significant ideas included hobcarts for spina bifida children, retarder braking systems for trucks, and domestic solar heating panels.[29] What they lacked was power to implement their plans.

Great potential for other socially-useful technology lies in proposals like this. For instance, computer systems are already being tested in efforts to harness off-shore wind power, as well as in their more familiar role in collecting solar energy. Community computing and community television provide other examples.

Those who raise critical questions about new technology deserve a hearing. Neo-Luddism may be limited by its class-based outlook. Ecological approaches may be suspect because of a dubious doctrine which values our oneness with nature above our being creatures of God. But if they ask at least some of the right questions — where are we going? what is this for? who decides? — they merit support.

Realism, not reaction, is required. To say this is to accept that jobs will be lost in some industries, and that skills may be lost in some jobs. It is to accept some risks attending the growth of information systems, satellite communications, and so on. But such developments are not seen as mere technical and economic necessities, as part of the logic of progress. They are assessed and channelled according to different criteria. The question is, *which criteria*?

A way of wisdom

It is time for poetry. T. S. Eliot once wrote:

> All our knowledge brings us nearer to ignorance
> All our ignorance brings us nearer to death
> But nearness to death, no nearer to God.
> Where is the life we have lost in living?
> Where is the wisdom we have lost in knowledge?
> Where is the knowledge we have lost in information?[30]

He knew nothing of today's information technology. But he asks the right questions. As philosopher Hans Jonas observes, just at the moment when our technological capacity extends to the point where we can destroy the very basis of human life, we have dulled our senses to the voice of caution. Just when we realize that technological ethics must address long-term and global questions, we discover that we are not even sure of the ethic which once guided short-term and face-to-face relationships.

Is that ancient wisdom really beyond recovery, really irrelevant? Admittedly, it begins with humility, not hubris, with respect for God, not faith in ourselves, and thus grates with modernity. Without descending to special pleading, or canny contriving, let us ask honestly whether the Jewish-Christian ethic does not still seem salient.

Information technology touches our humanness at just about every crucial point. Think of automated decisions, artificial intelligence, and responsibility. Surely, as creatures made to be answerable to God and each other, we should struggle to retain responsibility at all costs. Think of robots, word processors, computer-aided design and tools. Is it not a basic human trait that we should be creative, skilful, and engaged in meaningful activity, as is the One whose image we bear? Dare we allow machines to demean us?

What of 'speaking the truth in love'? Can such open communication be maintained when some are restricted from access to its means, whether by cable TV or dataline? What of the liberating 'jubilee' principle, designed to prevent the accumulation of property and power in a few hands? Do we remain quiet about that in a world where the gap between 'information-rich and poor' grows daily?

How do we approach the question of isolation, or fragmented relationships, consequent upon 'telecommuting' and high-tech careerism? Does this square with the biblical emphasis on the quality of relationships, of family, community, and love for neighbours? How can we think straight about digital deceit and mis-information technology? Don't some ancient proverbs remind us of a God who hates dishonest scales and prying eyes?

That ancient wisdom, whether mediated to us by Moses or by Jesus, certainly resonates with contemporary questions. IT affects the same human life as pyramids and ploughshares once did. The same wisdom affirms the technological project: it is a worthwhile human cultural activity! Men and women, as humans in partnership, are entrusted with opening up, with being stewards of natural and human resources for the benefit of all. Technology is a vital part of that activity. So 'technophobes' bark up the wrong tree!

Why then have I spent so much time in the critique of new technology? The answer is simple. We take on our technological responsibilities in a distorted context. Technofreaks are also misguided. The silicon idol binds us and blinds us.

So when we realize we are building a house on sand — the 'silicon society' — we must sound the alarm. Jacques Ellul says the appropriate response is to *transgress* technique, to desacralize technology. Expose the illusion that technical progress is spiritual progress! New technology does in many cases liberate us from drudgery, routine, and inconvenience, but never from selfishness, greed, dishonesty or domination.

Ellul rightly says we must ask 'what are the limits?', 'does the value of this new machine or system really justify the sacrifice or the risk?', and 'who will benefit, long-term?'[31] These are heresies to 'technological theology', whose basic doctrine is that 'if it can be done, it must be done'. This is why many of my comments appear negative. In the face of idolatry we are obliged to be iconoclasts! But it is silicon idolatry and its effects we oppose, not new technology as such. This is the tightrope we are obliged to walk.

Action in ambiguity

Technology is two-faced. A noble human activity on the one hand, but derailed and distorted by human waywardness, on the other. If we see only one face or the other, we are in danger of demonizing or deifying technology, of being either technophobes or technofreaks. This is the ambiguity in which our action is set.

Technology is not an independent force; the future is not foreclosed by technical or economic necessity. We hear politicians and pundits on 'the second industrial revolution' or the 'information age', but unless these terms are made to show us that *choices* confront us, they represent a lie. We fight the fatalism which says, 'the information society is coming, like it or not.'

Choices face us at every turn, from whether or not to buy the children a computer for Christmas (so I can play with it), to whether or not to install an office information network. An IBM advert depicts a man working at his desktop computer trailing one, and in the identical picture below, two cables across the floor. With only the power cable, he is working alone. With the network cable, he works with thirty-five (absent) colleagues. But what does that absence mean? Can the cable compensate for the trust and friendship of face-to-face co-operation?

We can only break out of that foreclosed future by dese-crating the idol, by insisting that choices are present. As Egbert Schuurman says, this does '*not* mean to throw tech-nology aside wherever possible. Rather, it means to appreciate technology's proper and meaningful place within culture and to develop technology intensively and responsibly.'[32] At the same time, it may mean we choose what Ellul calls an 'ethic of non-power'. That is, choosing *not* to do something simply because it is technically possible.[33] To spit in the eye of the idol.

My overall message is positive, and hopeful! Why? Because the ancient wisdom of a radical biblical perspective shows how technology may be practised in a liberating way, which anticipates a future worth working for. Because unlike the 'ancient wisdom' of Plato or Confucius, that of Jesus is personal, and contemporary. He *is* our wisdom, says the apostle Paul. In Jesus' life of love, in his reconciling death, in his return from the grave, he demonstrates wisdom which is not time-bound or partial. It exudes hope, secured by the resurrection. Without that, says Paul, faith is futile, and no lasting forgiveness, no chance of a new start, no disarming of idols, no hope for the future, is available.

Taking our cue from that basis of hope, we search for signs of hope which in some way foreshadow the new age. And because we are taught to love our neighbour, we struggle with the practical implications of that ancient wisdom, now. (Not much is heard about love in the silicon valleys of today's world. But there is plenty of fear. Fear of what might happen if we don't, and fear of what might happen if we do computerize. Love is the only known antidote for fear.)

Our ancient wisdom tells us to *ask radical questions*, but to *act in the real world*. We may question the whole economic growth and self-interest ethos of our society. But knowing we currently lack the consensus and will to slow the pace of economic growth and technological change, instead we salt the earth, grain by grain, in hope of its future transformation.

Who then will stand up for Michael Ducross, and for freedom of information? Who will plead the cause of Sharon Jones, isolated telecommuting homeworker? Who will help raise awareness of the effects of IT in the Third World, and give poorer nations a voice on appropriate technology transfer and a non-exploiting information order? Who will use their position in management or the union to encourage 'humanized technology' which co-operates with, not replaces skill?

Who will struggle towards greater partnership of men and women in new technology? Who will promote 'IT awareness' of an *ethical* and not only a skill-based kind, in schools, families, churches, and so on? Who will press for legal controls which allow maximum access to new information channels, such as cable TV? Who will develop them for appropriate ends, not just for more commercial entertainment? Who will insist on our making adequate 'human windows' so that people can 'see into' expert systems, such as those used in medicine or law? Who will support the signs of hope represented in organizations dedicated to pursuing social responsibility in computing and telecommunications?

The 'information age' holds tremendous technological promises, and parallel human threats. To secure the one and avoid the other requires a new ethical awareness as we make our technological choices. Having said that, I also believe that our ultimate hope lies outside technology, outside society, in the divine project Jesus called 'the renewal of all things'. Self-aggrandizement and destructive technologies will be transformed for socially-useful purposes — swords turned to ploughshares. And in the meantime? Our efforts in working towards that will be judged, not by headline successes, but by faithfulness to the ancient (but contemporary) Wisdom.

Notes

1 David Burnham, *The Rise of the Computer State*, Vintage Books, 1984, pages 33–34
2 *The Guardian*, 31 October 1985
3 *Practical Robotics*, July–August 1984, pages 61–62
4 David Burnham (see above), page 55
5 David Burnham (see above), pages 51–52
6 Figures from *The Observer*, 8 April 1984
7 Patricia Hewitt, 'What's in a file?', in Paul Sieghart (ed.) *Microchips with Everything*, Comedia, 1982, page 108
8 John Wicklein, *Electronic Nightmare: the Home Communications Set and Your Freedom*, Beacon Press, 1982, pages 198–99
9 Richard M. Neustadt, in Tom Forester (ed.) *The Information Technology Revolution*, Blackwell, 1985, page 563
10 *The Times*, 16 March 1985
11 *The Times*, 18 March 1985
12 *The Times Higher Educational Supplement*, 18 January 1985
13 This is mentioned, for example, in Michael Parsons, 'Theology and the Information Society', *Media Development*, 1983, page 34
14 Kenneth Baker, 'The impact of IT' in Bjorn-Andersen (and other eds) *Information Society: For Richer or Poorer*, North Holland, 1982
15 Dirk de Vos, *Governments and Microelectronics: the European Experience*, Science Council of Canada, 1983
16 *The Times*, 11 December 1984
17 Vincent Mosco, *Push-Button Fantasies: Critical Perspectives on Videotex and Information Technology*, Norwood Ablex, 1982
18 *The Sunday Times*, 5 May 1985
19 Quoted in Brian Jenner (ed.) *Future Conditional*, The Methodist Church Home Mission, 1983, page 59
20 Rob Kling and Suzanne Iacono, 'Computing as a by-product of social movements', in R. Gordon (ed.) *Microelectronics in Transition*, Norwood, Ablex (forthcoming)
21 Bob Goudzwaard, *Capitalism and Progress: a Diagnosis of Western Society*, Eerdmans, 1979
22 Jacques Ellul, *The Technological Society*: Vintage Books, 1964, page 74
23 Council for Science and Society, *New Technology, Employment, and Skill*, CSS, 1981, page 78

24 *The Globe and Mail* (Toronto), 9 August 1984

25 This study appeared in *The Educational Review*, and was quoted in *The Observer*, 18 November 1984

26 Judith Larsen and Everett Rogers, *Silicon Valley Fever*, London: Allen and Unwin; New York: Basic Books, 1984

27 See David Lyon, 'Ludd and chips: an appropriate response to new technology?' *Third Way*, March 1985, pages 24–26

28 Michael Shallis makes non-Marxist mileage out of the 'Luddite' critique in *The Silicon Idol*, Oxford University Press, 1984. Luddism is seen as a class-based critique in Kevin Robins, 'The political economy of General Ludd' in Liam Bannon (and other eds) *Information Technology: Impact on the Way of Life*, Tycooly, 1982

29 Mike Cooley in Donald MacKenzie and Judy Wajcman (eds) *The Social Shaping of Technology*, Open University Press, 1985

30 T. S. Eliot, from *Selected Poems 1909–1963*, Faber, 1963, page 147

31 Jacques Ellul, 'The power of technique and the ethic of non-power' in Kathleen Woodward (ed.) *The Myths of Information: Technology and Post-industrial Culture*, University of Wisconsin Press; London: Routledge and Kegan Paul, 1980

32 Egbert Schuurman, *Reflections on the Technological Society*, Wedge, 1977, page 22

33 Jacques Ellul (see above)

What can be done? Practical proposals

Having issued a challenge in this book, I ought to make some suggestions about how we may take things further. Three sorts of activity seem appropriate.

Raising awareness

At the most general level, we may all be involved in raising people's awareness of the issues discussed in this book. Within the formal educational process (in schools, colleges, universities) opportunities exist to develop relevant curricula. 'Computer studies' or 'IT awareness' classes should include consideration of the social, personal, and ethical dimensions of the new technologies. In schools especially, courses in religious education or social studies are good places to explore these further.

Within local churches, community groups and families, further opportunities may be taken to discuss the implications of new technology. From these discussions people could write to newspapers, or find radio and TV slots in which to comment on changing skills in local factories, how the disabled can be helped by new technology, or what are the effects of our new technology in Third World countries.

Computer users and enthusiasts could take spaces in the multitude of computing magazines, or even on computer 'noticeboards'. Social and ethical questions may be raised in many different ways.

Influence from within

A second kind of activity is to work towards shaping new technology within organizations and companies. Both managers, union members and others can use their influence to persuade people about the rightness of asking *ethical* questions about their activities. Can we shift our production to more socially useful areas? Can we increase public access to this database?

I talked with an employee of a chemicals transnational who was building an expert system to advise on when to spray fungicides on farms. He obtained approval to incorporate a more ecological approach than originally intended. The machine will now advise when *not* to spray, as well as conditions when it could be beneficial.

A further possibility is to use professional groups to encourage ethical approaches. This applies to librarians and information scientists, computing organizations and societies, as well as others *using* computers in education, law, and medicine. 'Information freedom', and 'human windows' are obvious targets for action.

Beyond this, your local library will tell you of other groups which operate to pursue these goals, such as 'Computing and Social Responsibility', 'Electronics for Peace' and so on. The 'social responsibility' sections of some churches are also engaging with these issues. A British example is:

The Society, Religion and Technology Project
The Church of Scotland
121 George Street
Edinburgh, UK

Applying pressure

Initiatives beginning either as 'awareness raising' or as 'influence from within' may end up being more accurately described as 'applying pressure'. Issues such as 'who controls cable TV programming?' and 'human windows for expert systems' are political as well as ethical, because they involve *public* accountability. Too often, as we have seen, new technologies are presented as 'technical or economic necessities'. We must apply pressure to put them on the political agenda.

Again, writing letters to city councillors, members of parliament, or of congress, is important. Pressure may also be applied through professional organizations, and through groups devoted to related causes such as world development (telecommunications and appropriate technology), broadcasting standards (content and access to new media) and civil liberties (rights of privacy, and rights to know).

Study groups who examine issues in depth can contribute their findings to relevant government committees at the policy-formation level. In Britain, one aim of the Shaftesbury Project is to stimulate just such activity. Its address is:

Shaftesbury Project
79 Maid Marion Way
Nottingham, UK

Glossary of terms

Artificial intelligence (AI): computers made to 'reason', using logical inference. Some say AI is *like* human mental processes, others that they *are* mental processes.

Alvey Report: British government report initiating a 'fifth generation' project, and advocating Japanese-style planning. It entails software engineering, expert systems, Very Large Scale Integration ('superchips'), and human/machine interfaces.

Cable TV: TV signals transmitted via a cable (co-axial or fibre-optic) rather than broadcast through the air. The 'wiring' is organized *either* as 'tree-and-branch' (where signals travel down a 'trunk' to the 'branches', homes or businesses) *or* as 'switched star' (like a telephone system, everyone is potentially linked with everyone else). The former is effectively one-way, the latter can be two-way, interactive.

Computer-aided design (CAD): using computers to aid the design/technical drawing process.

Computer-numerical-control machine tools (CNC): programmable machine tools (for cutting metal and so on).

Deskilling: a process by which jobs have their knowledge, judgment, or responsibility level reduced, for instance by automation.

Direct broadcasting by satellite (DBS): a satellite enables TV pictures to be transmitted over vast distances so that, for instance, one could receive American TV in Europe.

Electronic cottage: Alvin Toffler's (*The Third Wave*) term for residential accommodation with computers and telecommunications connections allowing remote working from home.

Eureka: a European high-technology initiative, proposed by France as an alternative to the military Strategic Defense

Initiative ('Star Wars') of the USA. Questions are raised about how 'civil' it really is.

Expert system: a computerized mimic of human expertise in a narrowly defined area, a 'computer consultant'.

Fifth generation: computers used for 'knowledge engineering', beyond the 'number crunching' of previous generations (1: vacuum tube computers; 2: transistorized computers; 3: integrated circuit computers; 4: Very Large Scale Integrated Computers). The Japanese have promised such machines, a thousand times more powerful than today's, will be available by the 1990s.

Information worker: term used to describe people who handle information, especially digital or electronic information. Tends to be loosely and thus misleadingly used.

Modem: small gadget which transforms binary signals (such as those from computers) into signals suitable for transmission lines (such as telephones).

New technology agreement (NTA): a fairly recent industrial relations innovation; management and workers negotiate the *way* that new technology is introduced.

Silicon chip: a very small sliver of silicon (made from common sand) in which is a tiny but highly complex 'integrated circuit'. Chips containing 250,000 transistors are in mass production.

Telecommuting: using computer terminals and telecommunications to work 'remotely', from home or from a telecommuting centre.

Value-added network (VAN): different locations are connected (for example, by renting telephone lines) or a service (like an information database) is offered for a charge.

Visual display unit (VDU): the screen or monitor used to see what is being 'done' with the computer or word processor.

Videotex: a two-way, interactive, text-on-TV medium. In Britain, 'Prestel' is the best known, offering a computer database from which information may be obtained using telephone lines.

Zap: To erase digital information.

Index